FOREIGN CYBER THREATS: SMALL BUSINESS, BIG TARGET

HEARING

BEFORE THE

COMMITTEE ON SMALL BUSINESS
UNITED STATES
HOUSE OF REPRESENTATIVES

ONE HUNDRED FOURTEENTH CONGRESS

SECOND SESSION

HEARING HELD
JULY 6, 2016

Small Business Committee Document Number 114–067
Available via the GPO Website: www.fdsys.gov

U.S. GOVERNMENT PUBLISHING OFFICE

20–701   WASHINGTON : 2017

For sale by the Superintendent of Documents, U.S. Government Publishing Office
Internet: bookstore.gpo.gov   Phone: toll free (866) 512–1800; DC area (202) 512–1800
Fax: (202) 512–2104   Mail: Stop IDCC, Washington, DC 20402–0001

CONTENTS

OPENING STATEMENTS

WITNESSES

APPENDIX

FOREIGN CYBER THREATS: SMALL BUSINESS, BIG TARGET

WEDNESDAY, JULY 6, 2016

House of Representatives,
Committee on Small Business,
Washington, DC.

The Committee met, pursuant to call, at 2:03 p.m., in Room 2360, Rayburn House Office Building, Hon. Steve Chabot [Chairman of the Committee] presiding.

Present: Representatives Chabot, Luetkemeyer, Hanna, Gibson, Brat, Radewagen, Curbelo, Hardy, Kelly, Davidson, Velázquez, Clarke, Hahn, Payne, Meng, Lawrence, and Adams.

Also Present: Representative Pittenger.

Chairman CHABOT. The Committee will come to order. Good afternoon, I want to thank everyone for being here. A special thank you to all our witnesses who came here to share their experience and their expertise with us here this afternoon. We very much appreciate it.

Small business cybersecurity has been a top priority for our Committee throughout this Congress. In our previous hearings, we have heard stories from small business owners who have been the victims of cyber attacks. We have also heard dire warnings from cybersecurity experts about the new and varied cyber threats facing America's 28 million small businesses all across the country.

There is no doubt that the information technology, or IT, revolution has provided small businesses with new tools and opportunities to compete in the global economy. However, we must be mindful that as small businesses use this technology, the risk of a foreign cyber attack has increased dramatically.

According to a recent report by Verizon Enterprise, over 70 percent of cyber attacks occurred in businesses with fewer than 100 employees, so small businesses. As we have heard many times, even one cyber attack can be devastating for small businesses, making prevention and protection absolutely critical. A 2014 survey from the National Small Business Association estimated the average cost of a cyber attack on a small business to be over $32,000, which is a huge hit for a small business.

Our Committee's efforts to spotlight these serious and growing threats have made it abundantly clear that the Federal Government needs to step up its game when it comes to protecting the cybersecurity of small businesses and individuals.

Today's hearing will examine the increased threats posed by foreign actors to American small businesses in cyberspace. This is an important dimension of the cybersecurity threat that impacts both our national security and our economic security, and I believe it demands much more attention than it has received thus far.

The FBI has already determined that foreign state actors pose a serious cyber threat to the telecommunications supply chain. It is also clear that many foreign nations are responsible for direct cyber attacks on the United States in an effort to steal intellectual property and sensitive personal information.

The Office of the National Counterintelligence Executive released a report in 2011 stating that tens of billions of dollars in trade secrets, intellectual property, and technology are being stolen each year from computer systems in the Federal Government, from corporations, and from academic institutions. China and Russia were cited as the two largest participants in cyber espionage.

In a report by our colleagues on the House Permanent Select Committee on Intelligence, U.S. businesses and cybersecurity experts have reported persistent attacks that could be traced back to China and were thought to be supported by the Chinese Government. Studies from the Department of Defense have warned of the difficulties associated with defending against threats posed by foreign nations, stating, quote, "means and opportunity are present throughout the supply chain and lifecycle of software development," unquote.

This is particularly troublesome for small businesses that not only rely on products from but also engage in commerce with globalized telecommunications firms from countries like China. Small businesses play an indispensable role in providing the Federal Government with products and services. They are integral links in the government's supply chain, but are often ill-equipped to combat against sophisticated foreign cyber attacks. This makes them a prime target for state sponsors of cyber terrorism who wish to undermine America's commerce and security.

I think we all look forward to hearing from our witnesses' assessment of this threat, as well as their suggestions for how we may better guard against this cybersecurity that we are discussing here today.

I ask for unanimous consent that our colleague from North Carolina, Mr. Robert Pittenger, be permitted to sit on the dais today and also ask questions in the order that we would normally follow. He will be at the end of the list of members that were here when we started, of course.

Without objection, so ordered.

I would now like to yield to the Ranking Member, Ms. Velázquez, for her opening statement.

Ms. VELAZQUEZ. Thank you, Mr. Chairman.

Over the past 15 years, the Internet and associated technologies have changed the way business is conducted. The Internet allows businesses of all sizes and from any location to reach new and larger markets, and provides opportunities to work more efficiently by using computer-based tools. It affords America's 23 million small businesses a unique opportunity to sell their products not only across the country but around the world. And while the Internet has fostered a tremendous degree of economic growth, it has also introduced profound security risks. Reports of massive data breaches have become commonplace, and the average cost of such breaches are devastatingly high.

Whether a business is thinking of adopting cloud computing or just using email and maintaining a Web site, cybersecurity should be a part of their plan. Theft of digital information has become the most commonly reported fraud, surpassing physical theft, and small businesses are the primary target. Just last year, 60 percent of all targeted attacks struck small and medium sized entities.

Among the worst threats to American businesses, particularly small firms, is cyber warfare performed by foreign entities. Not only are these cyber infiltrators accessing intellectual property and trade secrets, they are using the company's PCs to disguise attacks against other companies and the Federal Government. In fact, the Office of the National Counterintelligence Executive reported that tens of billions of dollars in trade secrets, IP, and technology are being stolen each year.

These actions have costly implications for small businesses and their ability to operate. According to research, 74 percent of small- and medium-sized businesses reported being affected by cyber attacks in 2011, with an average cost of $188,000 per incident and totaling over $2 million.

Combating these attacks have led to the U.S. Government issuing bans on certain foreign products and services, and also requiring small business contractors to meet demanding IT specifications. While these efforts are necessary, they prove confusing and costly to small businesses who are attempting to protect themselves and their customers from data breaches, stay globally competitive, and win Federal contracts.

Clearly, cybersecurity should be a priority to protect our national security and the economy. Failure to do so leaves all of us at risk. As we move forward, comprehensive reform must balance a number of priorities, including being able to adapt to evolving technologies, preventing undue costs and regulations of small businesses, and protecting our sensitive information.

During today's hearing, we will explore the critical issues facing small businesses that operate online and the resources they need to leverage innovative technologies. I look forward to hearing your recommendations to better educate and inform the small business community on cyber issues and how the Federal Government can facilitate a more robust and efficient cybersecurity environment.

I also would like to thank all the witnesses for being here and providing your expertise and have a broad discussion on this issue. Thank you, and I yield back.

Chairman CHABOT. Thank you. The gentlelady yields back.

If Committee members have opening statements prepared, I would ask that they submit them for the record.

I would now like to take a moment to explain our timing lights here and how we operate. We are under the 5-minute rule. It is pretty simple. You all will get 5 minutes and then we will ask questions, and we will limit ourselves to 5 minutes as well.

The lighting system is to assist you. The green light will be on for about 4 minutes, then the yellow light will come on to let you know you got about a minute to wrap up, and then the red light will come on and we would ask you to stop, not necessarily exactly at that point, but, within reason. Try to stay within those times, if at all possible.

I now would like to introduce our very distinguished panel here this afternoon.

Our first witness will be Jamil Jaffer, Director of Homeland and National Law Program at George Mason School of Law in Arlington, Virginia. He also serves as the Vice President for Strategy and Business Development in IronNet Cybersecurity. Prior to IronNet, Mr. Jaffer served as Chief Counsel for the Senate Committee on Foreign Relations. He attended the University of Chicago Law School, the Naval War College for a master's degree, and received his bachelor's degree from UCLA. We welcome you here this afternoon.

Our next witness will be Justin Zeefe, who is Cofounder and Chief Strategy Officer of Nisos Group in Alexandria, Virginia. The Nisos Group is a collection of former military and intelligence agency officials who specialize in cyber warfare, counterterrorism, and geopolitical operatives. Before the Nisos Group, Mr. Zeefe worked for the Department of Defense. He went to law school at the Boston University School of Law and earned his bachelor's from the Ohio State University. We welcome you here this afternoon, Mr. Zeefe.

Our third witness is Nova Daly, senior public policy adviser at Wiley Rein LLP in Washington, D.C. Mr. Daly specializes in international trade, cybersecurity, data and network security issues. Prior to joining Wiley Rein, Mr. Daly held senior positions at the Departments of the Treasury and Commerce, the White House, and the U.S. Senate. Mr. Daly received his master's in international law and organizations from American University and his bachelor's from the University of California Irvine. We welcome you here.

I would like to yield to the Ranking Member for the introduction of our fourth and final witness.

Ms. VELAZQUEZ. Thank you, Mr. Chairman. It is my pleasure to introduce Ms. Angela Dingle, Founder, President, and CEO of Ex Nihilo Management, a management and consulting firm that specializes in strategic assessments and information technology management. Ms. Dingle is a certified management consultant with over 20 years of experience in business leadership, IT governance, and risk management. She holds an MS in management information systems from Bowie State University and a BS in computer science from DeVry Institute. She is testifying today as a national partner for Women Impacting Public Policy, a national nonpartisan public policy organization advocating for and on behalf of women and minorities in business. Welcome.

Chairman CHABOT. Thank you very much.

Mr. Jaffer, you are recognized for 5 minutes.

STATEMENTS OF JAMIL JAFFER, DIRECTOR, HOMELAND AND NATIONAL LAW PROGRAM, GEORGE MASON SCHOOL OF LAW; JUSTIN ZEEFE, COFOUNDER AND CHIEF STRATEGY OFFICER, NISOS GROUP; NOVA DALY, SENIOR PUBLIC POLICY ADVISOR, WILEY REIN LLP; AND ANGELA DINGLE, FOUNDER, PRESIDENT, AND CEO, EX NIHILO

STATEMENT OF JAMIL JAFFER

Mr. JAFFER. Thank you, Mr. Chairman and Ranking Member, for inviting me and our panel here today to testify. I also want to thank the Chairman for his leadership on these issues. You know, you had a successful amendment recently, the State Department authorization legislation requiring the comptroller general to report on the State Department's potential use of devices and systems from cyber threat nations.

This is all the more important in light of FBI Director Comey's statement yesterday about the evidence they have acquired about the State Department's culture regarding the lack of security with respect to classified information, and in particular, the critical role the State Department plays in negotiations with foreign countries and the sensitive information they deal with from allies. In 2014 and 2015, we saw significant breaches of the State Department, breaches that actually led them to shut down their unclassified email systems and potentially expose classified—or sensitive data.

Now we are in a very evolving threat environment. The speed at which the Internet is growing is dramatic. 26.3 billion devices by 2020, almost three network-connected devices per person. There are a lot of opportunities and benefits that this environment provides to us. People in developing nations will have the opportunity to access information and markets they never had the opportunity to, and for people in developed countries like ours, we will have the opportunity to rapidly innovate.

Small businesses will be at the leading edge of that innovation. Startups in the Silicon Valley, from Chattanooga, Tennessee, to Northern Virginia, to various other places in the country are at the heart of this developing Internet environment. In our new economy, protecting our technology and our innovative edge is critical.

There are huge issues with cybersecurity threats today. The vast majority of breaches today, 75 percent by one estimate, are focused on the United States. That includes three out of the top five breaches last year alone.

We know about the cyber threats we face from nation—states. Countries like China are engaged in a constant and steady effort to siphon off our intellectual property for their own economic benefit. Russia is attempting to put in place efforts and programs for the next major conflict. North Korea and Iran have increasingly important cyber capabilities and are perhaps more willing than nations like China and Russia to use those capabilities.

We have seen in recent years the use of destructive cyber attacks. We saw Saudi Aramco in 2012 and Qatari Gas Ras attacked, roughly 30,000 computers bricked at Saudi Aramco. Here in the United States, at the Las Vegas Sands Corporation and the Sony Corporation last year, we saw cyber attacks where there were actual destructive efforts taking place, and that is a real concern.

The DNI, the director of the NSA, the FBI director, and the CIA director have all recently told us that cyber threats are the number one threat facing the nation, even exceeding the threat, as prevalent as it is, of counterterrorism.

Key to protecting our cyberspace is ensuring the confidentiality, integrity, and availability of information that flows through these networks. In order to do so, we must architect ourselves as a nation to defend against these threats, that means cooperation between the public and private sectors. Today, over 90 percent of the Internet is controlled by the private sector. We look to private sector companies to defend themselves, and yet in no other context do we expect the private sector to defend themselves against nation-state threats. We don't expect Target, for example, to have surface-to-air missiles on the top of their warehouses. To be sure, we expect them to have high fences, armed guards, and perhaps guard dogs, but we don't expect them to defend against a Russian bomber coming and bombing their warehouses, and yet we expect our private sector companies today to defend against the Chinese, the Russians, North Koreans, and the Iranians. We need to have a national conversation about how to defend ourselves.

Now, this is not to say that we expect the government to be on our networks at all times constantly protecting the nation with surveillance and the like methods. Nobody wants that today. To the contrary, we enjoy an open, free Internet, but we have to have that conversation about what the right role for the government and the private sector working together is in this modern threat environment.

In particular, China, we have talked about their IP theft, but one other thing we should really talk about is their desire to access key U.S. infrastructure. When I was at the House Intelligence Committee working for Chairman Mike Rogers, our Committee issued a report talking about the threat posed by Huawei and ZTE, two major Chinese telecommunications companies, to U.S. infrastructure. That report had very strong recommendations over 4 years ago about what the government and private sector entities should do with respect to Huawei and ZTE, and it is critical, as the chairman's amendment does, that we continue to look at this issue.

I would like to sum up by saying there are seven things that we could consider doing as a country, Congress working with the private sector, to address these issues. Number one, large and small businesses alike need to think about and get buy-in from their highest levels, board of directors to the C suite, down to workers about the need for cybersecurity.

Second, small businesses must consider working together collaboratively to share cyber threat information and use their collective buying power to address cyber threats.

Third, small businesses and large businesses must work together with the government to share information in real time and network speed.

Fourth, we need to get more serious about deterring cyber threats.

We need to make sure that the government gives more classified information to private sector entities. We need to consider positive incentives like tax breaks for investments in cybersecurity and information sharing.

Finally, if Congress is willing, we might want to consider amendments to the recently passed Cybersecurity Information Sharing Act to provide better and more incentives for cybersecurity information sharing.

That is just a short list, but thank you, Mr. Chairman. I know I am over time. I appreciate you taking the time.

Chairman CHABOT. Thank you very much.

Mr. Zeefe, you are recognized for 5 minutes.

STATEMENT OF JUSTIN ZEEFE

Mr. ZEEFE. Good afternoon. Thank you, Chairman and Ranking Member Velázquez and all Small Business Committee members, for the opportunity to testify on foreign cyber threats to American small business.

It is an honor to address members of this distinguished body, both as a small business owner and also as a citizen who notes that small businesses not only employ 50 percent of the private sector workforce in this country, but also produce approximately 50 percent of the non-farming GDP in the United States. They are, therefore, a vital part of the economy, and their well-being and the need to ensure their ability to operate in a transparent and secure environment is paramount.

My name is Justin Zeefe. I am Cofounder and Chief Strategy Officer of the Nisos Group, a cybersecurity firm in Alexandria, Virginia, composed of entirely former elite cyber operators and U.S. special forces officers. I and each of my associates have more than a decade of assessing and mitigating cyber risk to U.S. national security interests.

We each observed, over recent years, a shift by foreign cyber threats increasingly toward private sector concerns. This evolution, magnified by our observation that the commercial sector is wildly unprepared for this inbound threat, prompted us to bring our capabilities to industry.

It is also an honor to speak to you today regarding the most significant present and near-term threat to the national business economy: foreign cyber threats in the form of cybercrime. There are no shortages of statistics to this end. It is indeed the fastest growing economic crime, according to PWC, and is projected to cost the global economy $445 billion by the end of 2016. In fact, according to McAfee, the well-known security research firm, if cybercrime were a country, its GDP would rank 27th in the world, above Austria, Norway, and Egypt, along with others.

How would we collectively react if we knew that the 27th largest economy in the world was absolutely dedicated to attacking our value? What if they were overwhelmingly directing their actions against small business here in the United States? In fact, if you turn both of those into statements, they would be accurate.

Symantec, another very well respected research firm, found in June of 2015 that 75 percent of cyber attacks were directed at organizations with fewer than 2,500 employees, a dramatic increase from years prior. Not a week goes by that we don't read about a major data breach in the paper, with mention of what the attackers stole and often how they managed to gain access.

Most voices and solutions in the field of cybersecurity address the what and the how of the threat, yet without an intimate understanding of the threat actors, their motivations, vulnerabilities, capabilities, intent, and adaptability, the discussion is really incomplete. Never in the history of mankind has there been an industry, illicit or otherwise, which could be addressed strategically without factoring in the players of the game. Cybercrime and the threat it represents against small business and large alike is no outlier.

This very thing, the why, is a vital part of the equation, which requires understanding the humans behind the threat and, just as importantly, the vulnerabilities which these threat actors seek to exploit. By understanding the driving forces and motivations behind the threat actors, as well as the evolution of their tools, it is possible to narrow the gap between threat actor capability and cybersecurity solutions in the marketplace.

Once we understand those threat actors and their motivations, it becomes easier to model future behavior from state-sanctioned or state-sponsored activity and criminal enterprise, the source of almost all cyber incidents. Armed with these insights, only then should we deliberately consider legislative incentives, penalties, and appropriate distribution of risk to aid, not hamper, small business.

So, why? Why do foreign cyber threats target small business? One word and one analogy are sufficient to encapsulate this trend. The word is "profit." The analogy is that like water or electricity, malicious actors follow the path of least resistance.

As larger organizations professionalized their defensive and reactive posture to cyber incidents, and as stolen data became less profitable due to stricter regulatory and law enforcement environments, threat actors in search of profit turned the focus of their targets to small business, which had neither the capacity nor the budget to address this threat. A positive feedback loop ensued, and continues to this day, in which threat actors become only more dangerous as they adapt to this sophisticated target set and the unsophisticated target set alike.

The first and most significant evolution was the professionalization of the threat actor. What only a few years ago was best described as small bands of hackers who occasionally worked together have, by virtue of their success, drawn the attention of traditional organized crime. These groups, with many years of experience in the conduct of criminal enterprise, accurately assessed that cybercrime represented an opportunity for increased profit and decreased risk. Rather than trafficking in weapons, drugs, or other contraband as they had been accustomed, activities dependent on physical items, which present a significant risk of detection or interdiction, these groups of experienced criminals increasingly invest in individuals or groups whose cybercrime activities are wildly successful and stealthy when it comes to attribution.

In conclusion, it is vital that we not only consider the what and the how, but the why and the actors behind these incidents. Thank you for your time.

Chairman CHABOT. Thank you very much.

Mr. Daly, you are recognized for 5 minutes.

STATEMENT OF NOVA DALY

Mr. DALY. Thank you, Mr. Chairman and Ranking Member Velá zquez and members of this Committee. Thank you very much for the opportunity to appear before you today.

Today, I offer my perspective on cybersecurity broadly and distinctly as it pertains to small business. My perspective is drawn from experience as a former official with the U.S. Department of Treasury helping administer the Committee on Foreign Investment for the United States, which saw much cybersecurity transactions; with the National Security Council helping with not only trade and investment, but also cyber policy; and also in the private sector working with my colleagues to help small businesses confront the cybersecurity threats that are out there.

As this Committee knows very well, cybersecurity issues are clearly significant and growing economic risks for all small businesses, and Americans broadly. These issues have become increasingly relevant as we now depend on Internet access and connectivity in nearly every aspect of our work and lives, from the communication devices and processing devices we use at home and at work, to the vehicles we drive, the infrastructure we depend on, and even the appliances in our home.

It has been forecast that, on average, 5.5 million new devices are connected to the Internet each day, and that by 2020, over 20 billion devices will be connected to the Internet. For small businesses, the very connectivity that allows for greater freedom and versatility in conducting day-to-day business, linking phones, computers, routers, copiers, even alarms and ventilation systems, also brings with it significant and sometimes paralyzing risk, risk that is often difficult to address both financially and in terms of human resources.

As small businesses increase their connectivity to the Internet, they face significant challenges, not just in infrastructure and the nuts and bolts of establishing business connectivity, but also in security-related costs. Both domestic and foreign criminals, as well as foreign governments, have been known to exploit and are even actively targeting Internet-based vulnerabilities in order to gain access to financial information, customer data, and intellectual property. Three years ago, a study issued by the Center for Strategic and International Studies estimated that the annual cost of cybercrime in the U.S. was $1 billion. According to more recent reports, cybercrime costs quadrupled since then and are even going to quadruple into 2015 to 2019.

While large businesses typically have the means to fund and invest in strong and resilient cybersecurity measures to protect their interests, small businesses generally do not have this luxury. They often lack the capabilities or the resources to pursue strong entity-wide cyber protections. Further, small businesses often may not be privy to the kinds of broad industry-wide threat notifications to which larger companies may be. Often, larger companies have the resources to continually monitor and review threats that may arise from certain technology and supply chains, and at times are contacted by the U.S. Government when breaches occur. A notable example was a 2014 Department of Justice investigation and prosecution of several Chinese military officials who were responsible for breaches of numerous U.S. companies' security perimeters. There, at least some of the affected companies were contacted and alerted while the breaches were occurring.

However, given the breadth of existing cyber threats and continued growth of our cybercrime, our government simply does not have the resources to address all the cybersecurity-related issues faced by businesses, critical infrastructure, and government systems, let alone those faced by small business.

In 2012, the House Permanent Select Committee on Intelligence issued a report on its findings regarding security threats posed by certain telecommunications companies doing business in the United States. Despite the report's negative findings, the companies investigated continue to grow as dominant players in the global technology market. While it has been effectively restricted from selling network equipment to Tier 1 carriers, Huawei is growing its sales to smaller wireless U.S. carriers, supplying network infrastructure equipment to cities in the States of Washington and Oregon, and is targeted to continue growth in cell phone sales. Last year, ZTE was the fourth largest smartphone vendor in the United States, with 7.2 percent market share. Both these companies were notably sanctioned for export control violations.

Although much larger U.S. companies can engage other vendors and many vendors to provide certain cybersecurity monitoring and reinforcement of their perimeters, small businesses don't have the funds or capacity to do so.

While doing business with such companies can present heightened risk, it should not be overlooked that there is significant and growing vulnerability within the entire U.S. technology supply chain. Increasingly, our technology communications equipment and systems are produced or assembled abroad, and we are seeing nations taking strong measures to grow their own semiconductor and technology industries. Further, the United States is finding itself with a talent shortage in cybersecurity.

So how do we deal with this issue? I present a couple ideas or perspectives or views. First, focus on current laws. Enforcement is key. We should continue to do so and send signals to the market and to the private business and small business.

Promote cyber standards. We should consider frameworks such as ISO standards to promote best practices.

We should engage small businesses not only in education and outreach, but also in funding. A bill that was introduced, H.R. 5064, the Improving Small Business Cybersecurity Act of 2016, would be an important end.

Lastly, we have to address the supply chain security issues in the United States and close the cyber deficit. As I mentioned earlier, our supply chains and much of our equipment is being produced abroad. If we lose the capabilities and talents, not only in cybersecurity, but also in our capabilities of technology, we will lose our edge and our innovation.

Thank you very much for this time.

Chairman CHABOT. Thank you very much.

Ms. Dingle, you are recognized for 5 minutes.

STATEMENT OF ANGELA DINGLE

Ms. DINGLE. Thank you, Chairman, Ranking Member Velázquez, and distinguished members of the Committee. Thank you for the opportunity to testify.

My name is Angela Dingle. I am the president and CEO of Ex Nihilo, a woman-owned small business based in Washington, D.C., that provides cybersecurity, IT governance, and risk management services to government agencies. I am here today representing Women Impacting Public Policy, which is a national nonpartisan public policy organization advocating on behalf of women entrepreneurs.

First, I would like to thank the Committee for holding this hearing. Few topics are as timely as today's hearing.

The National Cybersecurity Alliance found that 60 percent of businesses will close within 6 months of a cyber attack. Narrowing the focus, businesses that work with the Federal Government are an additional security risk, given that the U.S. Government's research data and engineering specifications are of high value to individuals, companies, and governments across the world. Due to increasing privacy requirements and recent cybersecurity attacks, the Department of Defense responded by implementing new contract requirements.

In August of 2015, DOD finalized a regulation requiring companies of all sizes to safeguard unclassified, controlled technical information that resides on their information systems. The goal of the rule is to provide minimum standards to protect government information that finds its way into contractor information systems. The guidelines include 14 families of security requirements, commonly known as security controls or security objectives, that must be satisfied. These groupings range from identification and authentication, to physical protection.

Contractors that do not implement safeguards for the 14 families must submit a written explanation of why the required security control is not applicable or explain how an alternative control or protective measure is being used to achieve the same level of protection.

This past February, the SBA Office of Advocacy found that this DOD rule grossly underestimated the number of affected small businesses. The cost of compliance with this rule will be a significant barrier to small businesses engaging in the federal acquisition process.

Even more concerning is the May 2016 National Industrial Security Program Operating Manual, or NISPOM, Conforming Change 2, commonly referred to as the insider threat program. This regulation stems directly from concerns over contractor employees' ability to bypass security safeguards. The rule requires contractors to gather, integrate, and report relevant credible information that may indicate a potential or actual insider threat. It is especially burdensome for small businesses because it has to be implemented by November 30, 2016. WIPP is particularly concerned about the significant burdens associated with these new requirements and their potential to push women-owned firms out of the federal market.

Lack of technical knowledge is not an excuse for failure to comply with basic cybersecurity regulations. Small businesses need to proactively understand the scope and impact of changes on the business; align organizational policies, practices, and procedures to comply; empower those with the technical expertise necessary to implement changes; provide adequate training to ensure employees are aware of their responsibilities; and hold individuals accountable for compliance.

The first step is to get a jump start on the new requirements by assessing current information systems and determining changes necessary for compliance with new guidelines. Implementing effective governance processes can help small businesses manage information security risks, increase stakeholder confidence, and reduce the costs associated with compliance. To that end, small businesses could use assistance in determining their cybersecurity needs.

WIPP supports Representative Hanna's H.R. 5064, which was included in this year's National Defense Authorization Act. The legislation authorizes small business development centers to support small businesses in developing affordable cybersecurity plans. However, we would encourage the Committee to consider adding other SBA resource partners, including over 100 women's business centers.

In conclusion, women entrepreneurs consider the federal marketplace a key opportunity to grow their businesses. While there is a need to protect federal data and small businesses need to protect themselves from cyber attacks, the government has gone too far with new regulations. One size did not fit all. Ensuring that new cybersecurity requirements are attainable for small business is of paramount importance. This Committee has always acted in a bipartisan manner to support women entrepreneurs, and we appreciate your examination of this issue.

Thank you for the opportunity to testify, and I am happy to answer any questions.

Chairman CHABOT. Thank you very much.

We will now move into the questioning part, and I will recognize myself for 5 minutes.

Mr. Jaffer, I will begin with you. When a foreign company is caught stealing data or information from another entity, what are the common enforcement mechanisms available and what recommendations would you make to improve on those enforcement mechanisms in order to further deter foreign cyber attacks?

Mr. JAFFER. Sure. Mr. Chairman, part of the challenge, as you know, with foreign companies stealing U.S. information is our ability to get jurisdiction over them, and particularly if they are state actors. State actors are particularly the most problematic, whether it is China or its proxies or other nation—states, stealing our information is something we have got to critically address.

The best way to deter nation states from doing it, whether they are operating through their companies or not, is to have a deterrence policy. The key elements of a deterrence policy are, one, describing what our capabilities are; describing how we might use them, if and when we have information stolen or attacks made on our country; and then actually carrying those out, and part of it is credibility. So that is one of them.

In addition, we obviously have the ability to prosecute folks, but we have got to be able to get jurisdiction over them. That is the really hard part.

Chairman CHABOT. Thank you very much.

Mr. Zeefe, I will move to you next. You had mentioned, why are so many small businesses in particular targeted, and you said it is because of profit, it is the least resistance is among small business folks. What are a few things that small business folks who may be watching or may hear about the hearing or that we may correspond with, what are some things practically that they could do, as small businesses, to protect themselves from cyber attacks?

Mr. ZEEFE. Thank you. The majority of threat actors operating today are operating for profit, as mentioned. The best thing that a small business could do is ensure that their network is relatively secure by following the protocols that are standard across all industry; that is, ensuring that you have configured your network correctly, ensuring that you are encrypting your most sensitive data when possible, not being lax when it comes to security, ensuring that your password management is reasonable, ensuring that the folks who have administrator access on your domain do not use the same password there as they do at their gymnasium or anywhere else that might be hacked, as very regularly these hacks come through third-party incidents. So it is not that your business is hacked, but rather that a third party is hacked, I gain credentials to your business and I use them.

Chairman CHABOT. Thank you very much.

Mr. Daly, I will move to you next, if I can. What are, and this is somewhat related to what I just discussed with Mr. Zeefe, some of the common mistakes that you see made by small business folks that leave them vulnerable to cyber attacks?

Mr. DALY. I think it is not providing the education within their own workforce to let their employees know the vulnerabilities that are out there, in terms of making sure their passwords are protected, making sure the systems are protected in the way they operate it. So I think it is that employee knowledge.

Also, in terms of not necessarily the equipment, but making sure they have the right software, making sure it is updated, and continuously taking sort of a proactive approach to the cybersecurity that they provide their systems.

Chairman CHABOT. Thank you very much.

Ms. Dingle, let me ask you this. When you started off, it struck me that you said 60 percent of businesses, I guess small businesses in particular, close within 6 months of a cyber attack. I had mentioned in my opening statement that the average loss is about $32,000 that a business suffers.

Do you want to expound upon why such a large number do go out of business when there is a cyber attack? Are there any stories or cases in particular that you would want to let us know about? Ms. DINGLE. Certainly. As many of the panelists here have spoken about, the cost of responding to a cybersecurity breach is very expensive. As this Committee may be aware, small businesses don't necessarily have the financial means. They don't necessarily have reserves that they can quickly allocate to address a cybersecurity breach. The cost of having to pay for outside expertise to come in, help investigate and identify the actual problem that has occurred, and mitigate that can be very expensive, and that is why they end up going out of business.

I personally know of small businesses who, like some of the other panelists have spoken about, just did not understand what it takes to properly secure their business, only to be hacked or to have a security breach, and have had to tap a number of different resources that one would tap to finance your business for payroll or other sources to try to combat these cybersecurity issues.

Chairman CHABOT. Thank you very much.

My time has expired.

The gentlelady from New York, the Ranking Member, is recognized for 5 minutes.

Ms. VELAZQUEZ. Thank you, Mr. Chairman.

Ms. Dingle, as you mentioned before, the DOD, NASA, and GSA recently issued rules pertaining to all future federal contracts, which require a contractor to implement a set of cybersecurity measures to safeguard information, and more agencies will continue to identify and prioritize cyber standards.

What can we do to ensure that small contractors are involved in this process as uniform cybersecurity guidelines are developed?

Ms. DINGLE. Thank you. It is really important that small businesses have education sources. A lot of times these discussions are happening in environments where small businesses don't necessarily have a representative or a presence, and the Federal Acquisition Council may be having discussions about the timing of when these will be implemented. Although there was research that was done about that DOD rule, as the owner of a federal contractor, we certainly were not questioned about how timely we thought the requirements should be with respect to our ability to comply.

I think education is really important, and allowing the small business resource centers to provide that education would be extremely helpful to small businesses.

Ms. VELAZQUEZ. Do you see any active role being played by the Small Business Administration to make sure that small businesses understand the risks so that they could implement cybersecurity measures?

Ms. DINGLE. In the last 12 months, I have seen webinars and other information that the SBA has tried to make available to small businesses. But, again, depending on how small the business is, finding the time to participate in those and to stay ahead of and abreast of those is really what is difficult. Partnerships between the SBA and resource centers and organizations such as WIPP to educate small businesses is what I think would really be beneficial to them.

Ms. VELÁZQUEZ. Thank you.

Mr. Jaffer, federal spending to combat cybercrime continues to grow at an extremely rapid rate. What steps can be taken to tap the unique talents of nimble small technology firms in an effort to strengthen our national security defenses?

Mr. JAFFER. Thank you, Ranking Member Velázquez. I think that is exactly right. We have to tap the resources that startup companies in the Silicon Valley and across the nation have, the innovative ideas to address concerns that the Federal Government has, but the Federal Government is challenged when it comes to buying from small startups. There are all these regulations, that Ms. Dingle correctly talked about, that make it hard for small businesses to get in front of and actually sell to the government, even though they have some of the best, newest ideas.

We have to figure out a way to reduce that burden on small businesses and allow the government to buy from the most innovative parts of our community to address these very real threats. If we don't do that, we are never going to have access to that capability. It is unfortunate because the government, most of all, needs that access to innovative, smart, capable companies that are at the leading edge of cybersecurity technology. I think Ms. Dingle is exactly correct. We have to reduce the regulatory burden on those companies.

Ms. VELÁZQUEZ. Thank you.

Mr. Daly, nearly every single company selling technology to the U.S. Government and consumers, HP, Dell, Cisco, Apple, use foreign components in their products. Many of these products are used by small businesses. If there are any ill intentions, small firms are often not savvy enough to monitor foreign threats posed by these products or components.

What danger does this product integration within our market pose for small firms, and what is the best way to assist small firms in combating it?

Mr. DALY. Thank you, Ranking Member. I think the threats to our supply chain are very significant, and they permeate not only into large businesses, but our government systems and small businesses equally as well. So those vulnerabilities that the large businesses have, small businesses are going to have as well.

The issue is how to address that, as I alluded to, we have to think long term and structurally towards ways we can secure our supply chains, whether that be standards we are going to use in terms of making sure that the equipment is certified to a certain industry-held standard, and then that standard is something that the GSA complies with that will permeate its way into the private sector and flow down to private small businesses.

Ms. VELAZQUEZ. Thank you. I yield back.

Chairman CHABOT. Thank you. The gentlelady's time has expired.

The gentleman from Missouri, Mr. Luetkemeyer, who is the Vice Chairman of this Committee, is recognized for 5 minutes.

Mr. LUETKEMEYER. Thank you, Mr. Chairman.

Mr. Jaffer, you made some interesting comments, and I appreciate you being here today. You were talking a minute ago with regards to the small businesses being attacked and the venues for going after the attackers. I want to focus on the small business, because I think you were talking mainly about the government side of this, but I want to talk about the small business guys.

If you have a small business out there and they get attacked by a hacker, where do they go? Who is the law enforcement agency that they need to go to, talk to, to get some sort of restitution? Is it possible, because I think a comment was made a minute ago with regards to tracking these people down, and if it is a government-sponsored hack, how do you go after something like that? Can you elaborate a little bit on that?

Mr. JAFFER. Sure. Thank you, Mr. Vice Chairman. The first responder in these circumstances typically is the FBI. Small businesses and large businesses should go to the FBI. The challenge we have as a government, though, is you have DHS out there talking about its capabilities, you have FBI, you have DOD, and everyone is talking about the role they play. We as a government, haven't done a very good job of bringing that together and telling the private sector, particularly small businesses, who the lead is.

When it comes to investigations, I think the Bureau is the first place to go, at the local field office. The FBI is engaged in an effort to build bridges, but they are typically doing it with large companies. We need to figure out how to get small businesses, particularly private sector small business resource centers, like Ms. Dingle highlighted, and get the FBI and other agencies in with that part of the community to better address their concerns when they are hacked.

Mr. LUETKEMEYER. Do we have the ability and have you seen cases where we actually win against the bad guys, we catch the bad guys and then the small business gets restitution for whatever IP they have lost?

Mr. JAFFER. I am not aware of specific examples. I know that we have prosecuted folks and put them in jail. Getting actual restitution may be harder, and it may be an opportunity for Congress to consider legislation to create a cause of action to allow going after foreign cyber threat actors for restitution with stolen IP.

Mr. LUETKEMEYER. Okay. So right now, because there is limited ability to get restitution, the small business is sitting there basically on its own if it gets hacked, hopefully the information is not such that it is going to drive it out of business.

Mr. JAFFER. One area to think about might be sanctions collections and look at that as a potential pot of money that is here domestically that might be accessed by small businesses and other folks that are hacked by foreign nation-state actors or foreign companies.

Mr. LUETKEMEYER. Very good.

Mr. Daly, you talked a minute ago about a talent shortage in cybersecurity. It is interesting, because today in the Washington Times commentary section is a story titled Meeting the Cyber Challenge. In the article it says, during the last 20 years, the size and skill level of the technology workforce has not kept pace with the demand for workers. Routinely, American companies and government agencies post more job vacancies than there are qualified candidates to fill. Over three-quarters of K through 12 schools do not offer computer science classes.

The article goes on to say that the Bureau of Labor Statistics estimates that almost 5 million jobs will be available in computing and information technology by 2024.

The gist of the article is to try and get Congress to spend more money and help bridge this technology gap. But we have a problem here that is recognized by a lot of folks, apparently, that we have a shortage of people in this field to be able to do the work to protect our companies, our government, and our assets from being hacked or being taken advantage of.

Where do we go from here? This is very concerning, because if we don't have the experts to be able to keep us in the lead, we are going to fall behind and then we are going to be in real big trouble. Do you care to comment?

Mr. DALY. I absolutely agree with you. I have talked to folks at Mandiant and Symantec and McAfee and others, and this is something that is very apparent, that we don't have the capabilities to deal with this sort of knowledge-base gap in cybersecurity.

I think you have to make market-based incentives that drive people to want to get that education, want to get those capabilities, and that is where people respond. Look, if they can get a great job, they are going to do the extra technology training, go to additional schooling to be able to have a job that is going to be very secure. Unfortunately, I took a recent trip and talked to three folks who are in college. They told me they were psych majors. I was, like, that is great, but, we really need to get back to the basics, focus on the technologies that are going to be core, and find incentives, market-based incentives to get us there.

Mr. LUETKEMEYER. Thank you.

I yield back the balance of my time.

Chairman CHABOT. Thank you. The gentleman yields back.

The gentlelady from North Carolina, Ms. Adams, who is the Ranking Member of the Investigations, Oversight, and Regulations Subcommittee, is recognized for 5 minutes.

Ms. ADAMS. Thank you, Mr. Chair, and thank you, Ranking Member Velázquez, for hosting the hearing today. Thank you all for your testimony.

My first question, Mr. Jaffer, it seems like most cybersecurity solutions are geared toward larger companies, leaving small- and medium-sized enterprises vulnerable to cyber criminals and hackers. What options are there for small businesses that want to protect themselves but have limited resources?

Mr. JAFFER. Yes, ma'am. That is a great question. One opportunity that small businesses could take is to band together in associations or the like to use their purchasing power to buy larger scale cybersecurity solutions, have perhaps common security operations centers. A lot of big companies have these amazing rooms with big flat screen TVs, and they are looking at all the cyber threats and confronting them. Small businesses don't have the ability to do that, obviously. Maybe by banding together through their associations they can buy that capability from larger companies and work collectively.

Ms. ADAMS. Okay. One issue for small firms is the theft of intellectual property. This type of crime can be devastating to small firms and will result, as has been said, with many of them going out of business. How can IP theft, particularly from small businesses, hurt our economy and national security?

Mr. JAFFER. Again, I think you are absolutely right. It is a totally crushing threat, particularly for small businesses, but net net for our larger economy. As we shift to this technology-driven industrial and services economy, our economy fundamentally depends on our innovative capabilities and our ability to protect our intellectual property. If we can't do that—and today we simply aren't, China is taking it right out the backdoor in tremendous amounts—we have got to find a way to do that. That is a collective government and private sector problem. I think we have to address it for small businesses, as Ms. Dingle said, through the SBA and other organizations.

Ms. ADAMS. Thank you.

Mr. Zeefe, human error can usually be blamed for a fair amount of security breaches. How could setting a minimum threshold for cybersecurity best practices help small firms reduce the number of and severity of cyber attacks?

Mr. ZEEFE. The cybersecurity insurance industry has been setting the benchmark for that by creating checklists and essentially a punch list of things that an organization must accomplish in order to qualify for a policy, and then identifying and closing those loopholes which might trigger that policy or an exemption thereto.

Probably the best way, ultimately, is for both the small business community around the United States, as well as governments, to create a regimented checklist of things that organizations must do. Many of them revolve around human error, which incidentally is the vector by which the vast majority of these attacks are promulgated.

Ms. ADAMS. Could these best practices also help to reduce the burdens and the costs of keeping up with ever changing threats? Mr.

ZEEFE. They could. To your last point, they also have to be ever changing, because the methodology by which these attacks are conducted is shifting in response to our defensive posture. In order for us to stay ahead of the problem, we have to focus—in my opinion, we have to focus less on purely automated solutions and more on a hybrid of understanding what can be automated. That which cannot be automated has to be human driven, as the threat is entirely human driven.

Ms. ADAMS. Okay.

Ms. Dingle, implementation costs for IT security is of paramount concern that can cause small institutions to lose or even decide not to compete for bids against larger companies for federal and state government bids. In your estimation, what steps can be taken to ensure that small businesses don't have to choose between security and their bottom line?

Ms. DINGLE. Thank you for the question, and it is really an interesting one. In particular, entry into the federal marketplace can make or break a revenue source for a small business, and with these new regulations, very often a small business does have to make that choice. I think providing some balance between what is expected of a very large corporation and what is expected of a small corporation from a cybersecurity standpoint is going to be that balancing act.

Is it that everyone has to comply all at the same time, or to one of the other panelist's point, is it possible for small businesses to be able to band together to try to address those requirements? In particular, the DOD regulation that I mentioned earlier in my testimony requires that the small business itself handle some of those things. They have taken away that small business's ability to partner with either a contractor or with someone else to assist them in solving the problem. So just some flexibility in a small business's ability to respond would be helpful.

Ms. ADAMS. Thank you very much.

Mr. Chair, I yield back my time.

Chairman CHABOT. Thank you. The gentlelady's time has expired.

The gentleman from Mississippi, Mr. Kelly, is recognized for 5 minutes.

Mr. KELLY. Thank you, Mr. Chairman, and thank you witnesses for being here.

In my experience working with small businesses, number one, is the education or technical expertise of owners in this area is lacking. It is also very expensive in time, it is inconvenient, it is expensive in money. A lot of times small businesses use the hope method, which is, I hope I don't get attacked and they don't do that. It is very frustrating.

I am in the Guard and I have spent time with cybersecurity, also I was with the district attorney's office when I was there. A lot of the things that you have to do are extremely frustrating, especially to upper management old people like me who don't understand what these kids understand. We don't like changing our passwords, because we can't remember it. We don't like keeping things on separate computers because it is inconvenient. We don't like all the things that are necessary to do that.

That is across the board, whether you are military, whether you are civilian in small businesses, it is a cost. But the reality is they can't afford not to be prepared for this. I know that hard targets right now are going to be bypassed, because there are plenty of weak targets out there. How do we get this message across?

Mr. Jaffer and Mr. Zeefe, if you would answer this, how do we get this message across to our small business owners in a way that they understand, you can't afford to be a soft target, you have to harden up?

Mr. JAFFER. Mr. Kelly, that is exactly right. I think we have to figure out a way to ensure that small businesses get how critical it is to them. For them, at the core of their business is their reputation and their intellectual property, that innovative thing that makes them special and that makes them more competitive against these bigger companies. That is what makes them unique and makes them such a productive part of our economy.

Through the SBA and other organizations that this Committee has jurisdiction over, we have to strengthen them at the heart of their role as small business to protect that very unique edge. Without doing that, they are going to be much more vulnerable than larger businesses are, and that is a real problem.

Mr. ZEEFE. There are a number of policy prescriptions we could put in place to encourage, but ultimately, I suspect it will be an existential event or a series of existential events whereby a number of medium- or large-size companies have their reputations damaged or financial positions damaged to such a point that they go out of business. I think that will be the clarion call that brings some awareness to the table.

By and large, the reason that small businesses are being attacked with such aggressiveness is because they are so weak, because they are third-party providers to larger organizations, and because they can be squeezed for small amounts of money across the board. So as an attacker, I can go after 10 or 15 companies in an hour and extract $10- or $15,000 from each apiece far easier than I can going after a large financial institution and making an effort there.

So the short answer is, I don't know that there is much that can be done other than making this a public affair.

Mr. KELLY. Mr. Jaffer, again, I am a father, I have a young kid, and we all want to take work home, especially when we don't have the millions to buy multiple tools. A lot of parents take home their work computer and let their kids play games, or their work iPad or their work iPhone, and they let them use those. They don't understand that there is a danger of spillage. That is what we refer to in the military as spillage, it is when you take something from one net and take it to another net and expose it to threat.

Is there any way that you can think of so people understand that when you take either different classifications of information or when you have an intranet, and you expose it to the extranet—you know, you can't even use thumb drives on a lot of military computers and other things. How do we communicate this to let them know it is simple, but it is inconvenient?

Mr. JAFFER. Well, I think you raise a really good point. I have a 7-year-old, Nikko, and he plays on my iPad and my laptop; you are exactly right. He recently purchased a bunch of apps, so I learned about parental controls first hand. I think we have got to create separate accounts for our kids and for other family members that don't have access to those parts of the system.

Of course, hackers will be able to get through some those walls, but the higher we can build those walls, just at the very base level, keeping your system up-to-date, patch, creating separate accounts, that can help a lot. For small businesses, doing small things like that can make a difference. As you said, they are going after the weakest targets, and so we have to make ourselves stronger and not be the weak gazelle in the herd, as it were.

Mr. KELLY. I don't have to run faster than the bear. I just have to run faster than you.

I thank you, Mr. Chairman. I yield back.

Chairman CHABOT. Thank you. The gentleman yields back.

Mr. Jaffer, I hope you will encourage your son to go on the Small Business Committee Web site. I am sure he will find this fascinating.

Mr. JAFFER. As long as you have apps to purchase.

Chairman CHABOT. The gentlelady from Michigan, Mrs. Lawrence, is recognized for 5 minutes.

Mrs. LAWRENCE. Thank you so much.

Ms. Dingle, you stated that there were some webinars available for small businesses, but has the SBA proven to be effective in educating the small business owners and employers on the need to safeguard against potential threats? In your view, what are some of the recommendations you have had? I heard that we really need to get this going, and it is so critical. Can I get your opinion and recommendations?

Ms. DINGLE. Sure. Let me first address the latter part of your comment about whether or not people have been informed. Cybersecurity and information technology is a huge, huge issue. For companies that are not in the business of providing information technology products or services, it is a whole new world, for lack of a better term. If you have a firm whose day-to-day business is providing healthcare services or providing home improvement services, they are not thinking about technology.

The SBA, even if it is able to help, has to, first, make businesses aware that these regulations and the cybersecurity issues apply to all of us. I don't think that across the board people understand that this is a problem that affects us all. It affects us as individuals; it affects us as employees, as managers, and as business owners.

I am in the information technology space, so I don't look to the SBA for that assistance. I will tell you that I have not seen a lot of that, but that does not mean that the resources are not available. Trying to comply with the newest set of regulations, even though we are in the technology business, they are occurring so quickly that we have to bring in external resources to help us to comply with them all.

If there were small business cyber centers that were available, where we could go—and to Mr. Jaffer's point combine our resources to get access to the tools and technologies and expertise that we need to address this problem, that would be really helpful and beneficial.

Mrs. LAWRENCE. I just—I try to support small business, and they have these pop-ups I went to one of these pop-ups, and I saw something I wanted to purchase. The owner of this upcoming business said, I can't take a credit card. I have been hacked. She went over to a fellow pop-up person there saying, we are friends, can you pay? I found that very concerning, because here she is trying to start a business, and the pop-up industry is so exciting and really growing around America, and before she got off the ground, she had been hacked. It impaired her ability to take credit cards, because they had shut her down.

Ms. DINGLE. Indeed.

Mrs. LAWRENCE. The other question I have is to Mr. Daly. In your testimony, you mentioned strengthening information-sharing initiatives as a way to engage small business. Can you briefly talk about the organizations, we call them ISAOs, that were established by the executive order of President Obama in 2015, and is it enough, or what do we need to enhance it?

Mr. DALY. I think it was definitely very helpful, the work that it is looking toward making the SBA do, I think, is also very helpful. One of the intuitive things I draw from is one of the things we did at the White House. When we knew intellectual property was being stolen to such a degree, we did an entire initiative where we essentially ran it out of the White House pulling all the agencies together saying, look, can we do a combined initiative? It is called the Stop Initiative. We combined the resources of all the departments, made sure that they communicated, functioned, and had a one-stop shop for dealing with that issue.

I still think while it is helpful, that sort of initiative needs to occur.

Mrs. LAWRENCE. So, then, did it occur and stop, or is it still available?

Mr. DALY. It did occur. In terms of STOP, yeah, it did occur. At Department of Commerce, we have an IP czar that was established and continued. It led to a number of initiatives, not only creating a czar, but also creating commerce at a point, and was able to put new legislation as part of it too. So it was effective.

Mrs. LAWRENCE. Thank you.

Chairman CHABOT. Thank you.

Mrs. LAWRENCE. I yield back.

Chairman CHABOT. Thank you. The gentlelady's time has expired.

The gentleman from Ohio, Mr. Davidson, is recognized for 5 minutes.

Mr. DAVIDSON. Thank you, Mr. Chairman.

Thank you for you all being here and having some good information for small businesses and for our Committee. It is a pleasure to talk with you guys.

Ms. Dingle, one of my questions involves the National Institute of Standards and Technology framework. Are you familiar with that?

Ms. DINGLE. Yes, I am.

Mr. DAVIDSON. Okay. How have you found that to be—I think there was recently a review in April on how is that process going? What kind of impact is that likely to have for small businesses and industry in general?

Ms. DINGLE. The NIST framework that you reference does provide a framework for all things information security with respect to how you protect your information systems. There is an overarching 800-53 special publication that is revised on a regular basis, recently to Revision 4, and then there are associated special publications that have to do with various things that need to be protected. It is essentially the Bible that one needs to follow with respect to securing your systems.

The challenge, when you talk about a small business being able to comply with that, I talked about the new regulation for Department of Defense that had 14 families of controls. This one has much larger families of control to the tune to 2- to 300 things that a technical person would have to implement in order to secure a system.

In terms of a guideline, it is a very clear and distinct guideline on how one should protect information systems. It is just a very big, big, big set of regulations.

Mr. DAVIDSON. Okay.

Maybe, Mr. Jaffer, internationally, are there any technologies or practices that are not currently accessible or permissible here in the United States that are in use elsewhere in the world that would actually improve our cybersecurity here?

Mr. JAFFER. Thank you, Mr. Davidson. I am not sure—I am not aware of any specific technologies, but I do think that this goes to the larger issue about getting innovation into our system, whether it is foreign or American. We have got to find, particularly as a government, but also large businesses, ways to buy from the most innovative amongst us, the startups, those young companies.

I think, as Ms. Dingle correctly highlighted, it is a real challenge for small businesses worldwide to get into the U.S. Government sector. The U.S. Government needs our help. It needs the help of small, startup companies to get in there and give them innovative ideas. Whether it is international or the U.S., we have to figure out a way to make that happen.

Mr. DAVIDSON. Thank you.

In the assessment that you do, it seems like you do a bit of overall view of security. Is there a best practice that you would say, globally, if there is a country that really has a strong—that is actually connected to the grid—obviously, the countries that have no infrastructure maybe are more secure because there is nothing to be hacked. But those of us that choose to have access to the world, who has the best practices right now? If we wanted to say, is the U.S. a world leader or is the U.S. lagging, and who is leading?

Mr. ZEEFE. There are probably statistics. I am just using, what metrics I don't know, but I would say Estonia would be a surprising but accurate choice. They are the home of the NATO's Cyber Centre of Excellence. They are very careful to proscribe best practices to both their citizens as well as their companies that are formed from within the country. They take it very seriously, particularly as they have Russia on their doorstep.

Whether and where the United States would rank in that, to be honest, I don't know.

Mr. DAVIDSON. Not sure.

Okay. And then, Mr. Daly, just a question. In light of this week's news about the handling of confidential, if not classified, information and security, are there new laws that ought to be in place to make it clear that all of America, are subject to the Lady Justice, that there is no exemptions regardless of whomever you are?

Mr. DALY. I think that is a good and tough question. I think the laws, in terms of handling classified information, are fairly strong and you just need a Federal workforce that makes sure that it follows those guidelines strictly. When I had to handle that classified information, losing that privilege meant the loss of my job and a loss of confidence.

That public awareness is necessary. New laws, that is something that could be considered. Vigilance on what we have is always the key, so——

Chairman CHABOT. The gentleman's time has expired.

Mr. DAVIDSON. Thank you. I yield back my time.

Chairman CHABOT. Thank you. The gentleman's time has expired.

The gentlelady from New York, Ms. Clarke, is recognized for 5 minutes.

Ms. CLARKE. Thank you, Mr. Chairman. I thank our Ranking Member, and I thank our panelists for bringing your expertise to bear on today's subject matter.

I want to start with Ms. Dingle by asking, what would you say are the greatest barriers for small contractors wishing to break into the federal marketplace as it pertains to cybersecurity guidelines? Ms. DINGLE. Thank you for the question. For small businesses that are not familiar with doing business with the Federal Government, the Federal Acquisition Regulation, and in particular if you are talking about doing business with the Department of Defense, is a whole other language that they are not accustomed to.

Again, as I was answering Ms. Adams' question, if you are not in the business of doing technology, the fact that you have to comply with the cybersecurity regulations that are very technical in nature can be a barrier. There are essentially three types of security measures that one needs to put in place. One has to do with management and operations, the other has to do with technical implementations, so operations, management, and technical.

The average businessperson is thinking about how to manage and operate their business, but then you add these technical requirements on top of it. More and more often, when you submit a proposal to do business with the government, the requirements are already in the solicitations. If you are not able to comply, then you can't compete for that business.

Ms. CLARKE. What makes it difficult for small businesses to comply? Is it a financial? Is it a human resource issue? Is it a combination of both?

Ms. DINGLE. Yes.

Ms. CLARKE. Does the SBA have a role in assisting those who may be themselves qualified but do not have the capacity as designated in the solicitations?

Ms. DINGLE. Certainly, it is a combination of those things. It would be wonderful for new business owners, as you go to the Small Business Administration to get information about how to define your target market and how to learn about how different Federal agencies buy business, It would be really helpful if at that same time small businesses could learn about cybersecurity regulations, understand what their responsibility is, because that gives you the information that you need to make a decision about whether or not you can actually do business with the federal market and how great the barriers are.

It might be partnership with another business or teaming up with a larger business or holding off for a little bit of time until you can get the resources that you need to be able to satisfy all——

Ms. CLARKE. And build the capacity?

Ms. DINGLE. Correct.

Ms. CLARKE. So you would say there is a threshold that business has to meet in order to even offer themselves with respect to these solicitations?

Ms. DINGLE. Certainly. The more and more that we begin to focus on cybersecurity, it becomes a threshold; it is a barrier to entry.

Ms. CLARKE. Very well. Thank you.

Mr. Daly, what recommendations would you have for encouraging public-private partnerships to address the cybersecurity needs of small businesses, particularly those that contract with the Federal Government?

Mr. DALY. Yeah. I think creating standards with government procurement, it is amazing how those standards flow down the line to secondary providers all the way down to small businesses. If we set up a strong set of guidelines—for instance, there was a CGS appropriations bill that required certain measures to protect critical systems, NASA was involved in that, too, and that flowed down their entire supply chain.

Once you make those standards, the market responds to it. If we lift the water on our cybersecurity protections, I think all of those, including small business folks, rise with it.

Ms. CLARKE. So you are saying that the standards aren't clear right now? Are they evolving? Because, cybersecurity itself, that is a space that is continually shifting. How do we standardize a hygiene or a practice to the extent where a small business could actually sort of get in on the first floor?

Mr. DALY. As you said, it is an evolving issue of cyber, what the attacks and vectors are. But, as Ms. Dingle talked about, creating the standards that are out there that, the government response to in terms of its purchasing would be something that——

Ms. CLARKE. Just quickly to everyone on the panel. Do you think it is possible for a small business to be able to actually meet those standards and still be considered small?

Mr. ZEEFE. I do.

Ms. DINGLE. I do as well.

Ms. CLARKE. Okay.

Mr. JAFFER. I think it is very hard. I think we have go to try and find a way to lift that burden.

Ms. DINGLE. It is hard.

Ms. CLARKE. Very well. Very well.

I yield back. Thank you, Mr. Chairman.

Chairman CHABOT. Thank you. The gentlelady yields back.

The gentleman from New York, Mr. Hanna, who is the Chairman of the Subcommittee on Contracting and Workforce, is recognized for 5 minutes.

Mr. HANNA. Thank you, Mr. Chairman.

I am curious, what is the shelf life of security? We know it has some expense to get into it, but the theme here is that it is a cat-and-mouse, constant getting unsecure, getting secure, getting unsecure. What does that look like in the real world? What is the cost in the real world? What are the dynamics of that based on the size of your business? Along with that, what would be that kind of critical mass that everybody has to spend? Anybody that might feel comfortable.

Mr. ZEEFE. I would say relative to other forms of risk that enterprise, whether small or large, have faced in the past, cyber is relatively new. There is not a lot of actuarial data, whether you are looking at it from a regulatory or——

Mr. HANNA. But is it 6 months, a year, or a week?

Mr. ZEEFE. I don't know that you can put a bracket around either side of it. It is continually evolving. It is, as you said, a cat- and- mouse game. A more apt analogy might be, as you build a higher castle wall, I build a trebuchet. As you build a thicker castle wall, I develop, you know, air superiority.

Mr. HANNA. How do you manage that? Based on what you are saying, it is a moment by moment.

Mr. ZEEFE. It is, but really, all things offensive and defensive by definition have been. It is a matter of staying ahead of the threat actors and making sure that you are not the most attractive——

Mr. HANNA. But then the next logical question for me would be, is that doable, I mean, in the real world, with that kind of dynamic?

Mr. Jaffer?

Mr. JAFFER. Certainly for large companies, it is more doable than it is for small companies. The financial service sector is very innovative when it comes to defense, and they are constantly working together and evolving that. But that is why, we have to figure out how to get small businesses to work together. They are not going to be able to do this on their own.

One thing that Ms. Dingle mentioned was this notion of small business cyber centers. That is a really interesting concept, where the government might invest alongside a group of small businesses to get them a common operational capability and buy from some of the big vendors. It is an interesting idea. I have never really thought about it, but it is an interesting concept.

Mr. HANNA. Ms. Dingle, I heard what you said about women centers. I take it to heart and consider it.

Ms. DINGLE. Thank you. I wanted to address your question about whether or not you can, if it is a moving target, how do you ever try to address it? We answered our question about the NIST framework. You have to set some form of baseline, otherwise, you never get there from here, because the technology is changing so frequently.

I talked about the managerial and operational components of cybersecurity, and that really boils down to on any given day, if someone leaves your firm or you stop doing business with one of your partners, you have just introduced a new set of——

Mr. HANNA. So what you are really saying is it is a continuum?

Ms. DINGLE. It really is.

Mr. HANNA. And on that continuum, you can be at any point, and the goal is to be as advanced as you can be at any moment. As everyone here has implied and said directly, those people that are on the lower end of that food chain, if you will, are the ones that people go after.

Along those lines, Mr. Zeefe, I wonder if you could explain to me you said that someone would go into five companies and collect $10- or $15,000 apiece. How does that look? What does that look like in the real world? How would that be?

Mr. ZEEFE. At present, that is through Ransomeware.

Mr. HANNA. I hope nobody is taking notes.

Mr. ZEEFE. At present, Ransomeware is the attack, I want to say du jour, but it has really been months and will continue to be so in the future. That is effectively—are you familiar with the concept?

Mr. HANNA. Uh-huh.

Mr. ZEEFE. So for those that aren't, Ransomeware is effectively unlocking the doors of your organization, making it impossible for you to conduct business, and in exchange, I am trying to extract a modest toll respective to what your company is worth. It is my hope, as the attacker, that——

Mr. HANNA. Do people succumb to that kind of extortion?

Mr. ZEEFE. All the time. I don't have the exact statistics in front of me, but I believe it is over half a billion dollars.

Mr. HANNA. So I will give you back your system if you send me X amount?

Mr. ZEEFE. It happens all the time. And, in fact, quite regularly we see companies paying it, because the amount of money that they lose just for being down for a day dramatically eclipses the amount that they would have to pay to unlock it, reaching out——

Mr. HANNA. So nobody succumbs to the kill the captive thing? They always rescue the individual.

Mr. ZEEFE. No. In fact, there's been a development recently where it is getting kind of ugly. You have competing organizations out there, generally criminal in nature, affiliated with traditional organized crime, 85 percent plus, who are using tools that are copies of a copy sometimes. Their intent may be to release you after you have paid the ransom, but the practical effect is that they weren't very good at what they were doing, and therefore, even though you have paid the ransom, they are unable to unlock you. It creates some uncertainty in the marketplace of cybercriminal tools, which, believe it or not, is actually a pretty professional—— Mr. HANNA. That is a wake-up call for anybody who has to pay that. That person will respond, like Mr. Jaffer said, they go out and do what they needed to do to make sure it doesn't happen again.

Thank you. My time has expired. Thanks, Mr. Chairman.

Chairman CHABOT. Thank you. The gentleman's time has expired.

The gentleman from New Jersey, Mr. Payne, is recognized for 5 minutes.

Mr. PAYNE. Thank you, Mr. Chairman and Ranking Member.

Mr. Daly?

The export control system has long been criticized by exporters as being too rigorous, cumbersome, and inefficient. On the other hand, some argue that the defense and foreign policy considerations should trump any commercial concerns. How do you balance these two competing forces of increasing American competitiveness and American security as it pertains to cybersecurity?

Mr. DALY. It is definitely difficult. I know there is a serious issue going on right now in terms of encryption and what encryption technology can go abroad and its effect. Like anything, the devil is in the details and you have to be smart about it. You have to look at what is happening out there in the market internationally and say, are U.S. companies being disadvantaged, that their technologies are already being sold abroad? I know that BIS and the State Department are doing a lot to reform that system to make it not only commercially appropriate, but also ensuring that it protects national security.

So it is keeping that focus and making sure we are not disadvantaging companies where commercial technology is already available, readily available outside, but making sure we guard the crown jewels of the U.S. national security in terms of encryption technologies, and that just means being smart.

Mr. PAYNE. Okay. Thank you.

And, Ms. Dingle, the implementation cost for IT security is of paramount concern. These costs cause smaller institutions to lose or even decide not to compete for bids against larger companies for federal and state government bids. In your estimation, what are the steps that can be taken to ensure that small businesses do not have to choose between security and their bottom line?

Ms. DINGLE. Thank you for the opportunity to testify, and the answer to the question, I go back to my earlier comments about the small business' ability to combine forces to get either economies of scales or access to the resources that some of our larger competitors have. It can be as simple as having to buy a piece of technology that is $200 for you to purchase and use to access a federal system, or it could be as expensive as a half a million dollars to secure systems based on the NIST framework that I was talking about.

Anything that we can do to provide a set of resources that could be shared amongst small businesses or could be leveraged by small businesses to lower their costs and to decrease the timeline associated with implementation would be—would be very helpful.

Mr. PAYNE. Thank you.

In the interest of time, I'll yield back.

Chairman CHABOT. The gentleman yields back. Thank you very much. The chair is very appreciative of that, since we have votes called on the floor, and we have one more of our colleagues.

The gentleman from New York is recognized for 5 minutes.

Mr. PITTENGER. Well, thanks, Mr. Chairman. I appreciate the panelists.

A couple of different questions here. The first one is for anyone that wants to jump in, are there any telltale signs that the hack, is foreign versus domestic and what are the legal ramifications? Are they the same or might they be different? I heard earlier, we certainly got the recommendation, FBI is the initial entry point for the small business, but is that for both domestic and foreign? So let me just start with that one.

Mr. ZEEFE. I would like to address the nonlegal part of that question, the attribution question which you have raised. It is a good one and it plays into a lot of questions, predominantly the hacking back question which some people ask, can we go after them if we know who it was? Can we affirmatively ascertain who was responsible for the attack? The answer is, it depends. It depends on whether they intended for you to know who they were, whether they were very competent at what they were doing, and whether there is a reason for them to hide who they are.

The ability of a sophisticated attacker to effectively mask their identity or replace it with someone else's identity, it is difficult, if not impossible, to determine whether that is the case. So if you have been attacked and all of the signs are that it was somebody from Russia, that doesn't really mean anything. You have to get in there deeper, and it is less a forensic question and more of a human question. Is the pattern of coding that they used similar to what would be used by Russia? Or is it more likely Chinese or Romanian or somewhere else in Eastern Europe? The ability to understand who was attacking you is very, very complicated issue.

Mr. JAFFER. The answer to your question is, the FBI does operate internationally, so they can be a starting point. But they need to work better with the intelligence community, with NSA and the like, to figure out who is connected to these attacks. In particular, we have never really, as the government, made a good case for why the NSA can help the private sector. Part of what that is, we are inside of foreign government systems all the time looking over what they are doing and trying to take their information. One thing that could be useful for American companies is to provide some of that information back to the private sector in usable form to protect themselves. We don't do a very good job doing that. Information sharing is a good beginning point, but we need to do more there.

Mr. PITTENGER. The last question is really one I am inquisitive about, not necessarily in your inbox, but given your expertise, you may very well know. What are the requirements now for small business if they win a Federal contract? What requirements do they have in terms of briefings, compliance, accreditations as it relates to cyber, and particularly dealing with potential foreign attacks?

Mr. JAFFER. I think I will defer to Ms. Dingle on that. But, there are a lot, and they are hard.

Ms. DINGLE. Thank you. The regulations that are outlined in my testimony, they are new regulations that have come about in the last 12 to 24 months that have to do with protecting unclassified information, as well as if you hold a Department of Defense contract, those things are defined in the NIST framework and in the NISPOM. Essentially, you have to report any instances associated with that to the FBI as part of the burden that the small businesses are encountering, because they have to put a number of tools, techniques, and processes in place to enable them to be able to do so.

Mr. PITTENGER. I thank you, ma'am.

I apologize for being late. I was on the floor with our mental health bill. I don't seem to have your testimony. Maybe I can get that from staff in a little bit. I do have Mr. Jaffer's testimony. Perhaps they are just all out, you know, given the fact that I came late, but I do appreciate that input.

I can imagine for a small business, it is very daunting. So many things, so many balls to keep in the air and juggle, and then the prospect, the possibility of being hacked and then, first of all, what that means for them, and then also what that means for them in terms of their requirements. I appreciate you putting attention to that, and I look forward to reading that.

Mr. Chairman, thank you for this hearing, and I appreciate it. I will yield back.

Chairman CHABOT. Thank you very much. The gentleman yields back.

We want to thank the very distinguished panel this afternoon. Your testimony was excellent. Your answers, responses to questions are very, very good. I think it has been very informative for members on both sides here.

Ms. Dingle, what you said about 60 percent of the small businesses after being attacked go out of business within 6 months is particularly disturbing for those of us on this Committee who are doing everything we can to make America a great place for a small business to be successful. So thank you, all of you, for providing that information.

I would ask unanimous consent that members have 5 legislative days to submit statements and supporting materials for the record.

Without objection, so ordered.

And if there is no further business to come before the Committee, we are adjourned. Thank you very much.

[Whereupon, at 3:32 p.m., the committee was adjourned.]

APPENDIX

Prepared Statement of Jamil N. Jaffer[*]
on
Foreign Cyber Threats: Small Business, Big Target
before the
House Small Business Committee

July 6, 2016

I. Introduction

Chairman Chabot, Ranking Member Velazquez, and Members of the Committee: thank you for inviting me to discuss foreign cyber threats and the particular challenge they pose for American small businesses. I hope that we will have the opportunity to talk candidly about these topics and to discuss what we might do, as a nation, to confront these very real and serious threats.

I also want to note your leadership, Mr. Chairman, here in the House of Representatives on these important issues, and to highlight your successful amendment in the House Foreign Affairs Committee to the State Department authorization bill requiring the Comptroller General to report on the State Department's possible use of equipment and services purchased from suppliers linked to key cyber threat nations. The potential use of such equipment and services by the U.S. government is a key issue for congressional oversight, particularly given the threat environment that our nation—in both the public and private sectors—faces from nation-state actors and their proxies.

And, as we know from FBI Director Jim Comey's statement yesterday, the FBI has recently "developed evidence that the security culture of the State Department in general, and with respect to use of unclassified e-mail systems in particular, was generally lacking in the kind of care for classified information found elsewhere in the government."[1] This is troubling news indeed, given the important role that the State Department plays in our relations with other nations, the type of sensitive information it receives from our allies, and the critical nature of the negotiations it conducts on behalf our people. It is even more troubling because it comes in the aftermath of the November 2014 and March 2015 public disclosures of breaches at the State Department that prompted multiple shutdowns of the State Department's unclassified email systems and may have exposed sensitive data.[2] These incidents, taken

---

[*] Jamil N. Jaffer currently serves as an Adjunct Professor of Law and Director, Homeland & National Security Law Program at the Antonin Scalia Law School at George Mason University and is affiliated with Stanford University's Center for International Security and Cooperation. Mr. Jaffer also serves as Vice President for Strategy & Business Development for IronNet Cybersecurity, a startup technology company headquartered in the Washington, DC metropolitan area. Among other things, Mr. Jaffer previously served as Chief Counsel & Senior Advisor to the Senate Foreign Relations Committee, as an Associate Counsel to President George W. Bush, and as Counsel to the Assistant Attorney General for National Security in the U.S. Department of Justice.

[1] *See* Federal Bureau of Investigation, *Statement by FBI Director James B. Comey on the Investigation of Secretary Hillary Clinton's Use of a Personal E-Mail System*, Federal Bureau of Investigation (July 5, 2016), available online at <https://www.fbi.gov/news/pressrel/press-releases/statement-by-fbi-director-james-b.-comey-on-the-investigation-of-secretary-hillary-clintons-use-of-a-personal-e-mail-system>.

[2] *See, e.g.*, Office of the Inspector General of the State Department and the Broadcasting Board of Governors, *Semiannual Report to the Congress – April 1, 2015 to Sept. 30, 2015*, available online at <https://oig.state.gov/system/files/oig_fall_2015_sar.pdf> ("The Department spent approximately $1.4 billion on information technology (IT) in FY 2015. The same year, a number of cybersecurity incidents illustrated deficiencies in the Department's

together, simply highlight the need to ensure that the Chairman's amendment—or language to the same effect, perhaps even expanded further—makes it through the House and Senate floors and to the President's desk at part of the State Department Authorization legislation.

Stepping back, for the moment, from the challenges of internal government cybersecurity, however, may provide the members of this Committee the opportunity to examine the myriad and growing ways in which our nation—and the innovative small businesses that are key engines of job growth and investment in our economy—must confront the very real threats we face in cyberspace.

II. Cyber Opportunities

As members of this Committee well know, technology is rapidly changing. The amount of information circulating the globe via IP networks will reach 2.3 zettabytes by 2020.[3] This means that by the end of the decade, "the gigabyte (GB) equivalent of all the movies ever made will cross the global Internet every 2 minutes."[4] This growth in technology and IP traffic will be accompanied by rapid growth in the quantity of devices connected to IP networks, particularly as we move towards the so-called Internet of Things (IoT) environment. Indeed, Cisco estimates that by 2020 there will be 26.3 billion networked devices, or more than three IP-connected devices per person around the world, up from 16.3 billion such devices in 2015.[5] Traffic from wireless and mobile devices will also account for 2/3 of all IP traffic by 2020,[6] and the Internet Society forecasts that worldwide mobile Internet penetration will reach 71% by 2019.[7]

This growth in technology and connectivity offers huge opportunities and benefits for individuals and business around the globe. It will provide information access to oppressed populations and political movements worldwide. And it will also provide broad access to global markets and production capacity to businessmen and women who were once limited by geography or their national infrastructure. Indeed, Cisco estimates that IP traffic will grow fastest in the Middle East and Africa, coming in at a compound

---

efforts to protect its computer networks. Malicious actors exploited vulnerabilities, potentially compromising sensitive information and significant downtime to normal business operations."); *see also* Russell Berman, *The U.S. Government Is Under (Cyber) Attack*, The Atlantic (Nov. 17, 2014) ("The State Department on Monday joined the White House and two other federal agencies in confirming that it had been the victim of a recent and successful cyberattack. Spokesman Jeff Rathke told reporters at Foggy Bottom that officials 'detected activity of concern' several weeks ago targeting its unclassified email system and that it used a 'scheduled outage' to address the problem this past weekend."); Justin Fishel & Lee Ferran, *State Dept. Shuts Down Email After Cyber Attack*, ABC News (Mar. 13, 2015) ("The State Department shut down large parts of its unclassified email system today in a final attempt to rid it of malware believed to have been inserted by Russian hackers in what has become one of the most serious cyber intrusions in the department's history, U.S. officials told ABC News. 'The Department is implementing improvements to the security of its main unclassified network during a short, planned outage of some internet-linked systems,' State Department spokeswoman Jen Psaki said in a statement to ABC News.")

[3] *See* Cisco, *The Zettabyte Era—Trends and Analysis* (June 2016) at 1, *available online at* <http://www.cisco.com/c/en/us/solutions/collateral/service-provider/visual-networking-index-vni/vni-hyperconnectivity-wp.pdf>

[4] *See Zettabyte Era*, n. 3 *supra* at 4.

[5] *See Zettabyte Era*, n. 3 *supra* at 2.

[6] *See Zettabyte Era*, n. 3 *supra* at 2.

[7] *See* Internet Society, *Global Internet Report 2015*, at 9, *available online at* <http://www.internetsociety.org/globalinternetreport/assets/download/IS_web.pdf>.

annual growth rate (CAGR) of 41% between 2015 and 2020, with Central and Eastern Europe next at 27%, and as compared with a CAGR of 19% for North America over the same period.[8] And in the developing world, smartphones shipments are up, exceeding 50% of all mobile handsets shipments as of late 2014.[9] Not surprisingly then, regions like Latin America and the Middle East and Africa also saw the fastest growth in consumer mobile location based services worldwide between 2014 and 2015 at 62% and 52%, respectively, year-over-year. Similarly, mobile banking and commerce grew fastest in Latin America at a 49% year-over-year rate and the Middle East and Africa led mobile video growth at a 43% over the same period.

And it is not just developing economies that can benefit from these opportunities. Modern, developed economies will also increasingly rely on technology to innovate, to improve productivity, and to protect the fruit of such innovation and capitalize on productivity gains. Indeed, as the United States continues to evolve its core economic base towards a technology-driven industrial and services economy, protecting the core intellectual property that lies at the heart of such an economy will be all the more important.

Small businesses will almost certainly be at the forefront of this ongoing revolution. This is because, more than any other part of the economy, small businesses have the flexibility to create new products and to capitalize on advances in technology through rapid innovation and by bring products to market quickly. Indeed, it is this very feature of technology startups—which nearly always begin their lives as small businesses—that has turned the Silicon Valley and other technology centers like Silicon Hills (Austin, TX), Silicon Alley (New York, NY), Silicon Beach (West Los Angeles, CA), the Dulles Technology Corridor (Northern VA), Silicon Harbor (Charleston, SC), and the Gig City (Chattanooga, TN) into major hubs of productivity and technological innovation.

III. Cyber Vulnerabilities

At the same time, this reliance on high-velocity technological innovation and the creation of new intellectual property underlying the products these small, rapidly growing businesses are bringing to market, means that such companies, perhaps more than other parts of the economy, will be increasingly vulnerable to cyber threats. In particular, such companies are vulnerable to having the core of their business stolen out from under them: the particular innovations and associated intellectual property that they have developed to give them an edge in the global marketplace. Indeed, given that the primary focus of small business startups is often developing and bringing new, innovative products to market as fast as possible, it would not be surprising if, perhaps more than other companies, small business startups are likely to make security a secondary or tertiary focus.

This is not to suggest that major U.S. companies do not likewise face major cyber threats. To the contrary, the daily drumbeat of news stories about data breaches targeting major American companies across a wide range of sectors, from financial and information services to healthcare and retail, makes clear that a wide range of global threat actors are aggressively targeting our companies. One report estimates that 707.5 million records were lost worldwide, including accidental losses and malicious data

---

[8] See *Zettabyte Era*, n. 3 *supra* at 3.

[9] See *Global Internet Report 2015*, n. 7 *supra* at 30.

breaches, in 2015 alone.[10] Of these 707.5 million records, more than 60% were compromised by threat actors, including malicious outsiders (37%), malicious insiders (7%), hacktivists (4%), and state-sponsored actors (15%).[11] And while the overall number represents something of a downtick from the more than one billion records compromised in 2014, it is estimated that the total number of records compromised since 2013 exceeds 3.6 billion.[12] In 2015, the vast majority of the breaches—nearly 75%—took place in the United States.[13] And two of the top five breaches on the Breach Level Index, were American private sector companies in the healthcare and information services sectors, with a third being the massive U.S. government data breach at the Office of Personnel Management.[14]

According to Verizon's 2016 Data Breach Investigation's Report, which examined 2,260 breaches across 82 countries, in 93% of cases, it took attackers minutes or less to compromise systems,[15] a troubling static given the fact Verizon reports that in 83% of cases, victims took weeks or more to find out they had been breached.[16] Even worse, Mandiant reports that for organizations it investigated in 2015, the median time between compromise and breach discovery was 146 days (albeit substantially down from 205 days the prior year and 412 days in 2012).[17] Mandiant also indicated that on average, its "Red Team" was able to gain access to administrative credentials—essentially super-user access—within three days of initially gaining access to a given organization.[18]

Of the 64,000+ incidents and 2000+ breaches that Verizon examined, 16.3% involved insider and privilege misuse, 15% involved denial of service attacks, 12.4% involved crimeware (including ransomware), 8.3% used web app attacks (*e.g.*, e-commerce systems) typically for financial crimes, 1% involved point-of-sale or payment card skimmers, and only 0.4% involved cyber-espionage.[19] Most troubling for small businesses, 70% of the breaches involving insider misuse took months or years to discover.[20] And, while only a small percentage of the incidents and breaches involved cyberespionage, in the manufacturing sector in particular, nearly half of the confirmed breaches (47%) could be classified as cyber espionage.[21]

One of the key challenges facing corporate America today—and perhaps small businesses more than others—is simply making sure their IT infrastructure is up-to-date and that known vulnerabilities are

---

[10] *See* Gemalto, *2015: The Year Data Breaches Got Personal* (2016) at 3, *available online at* <http://www.gemalto.com/brochures-site/download-site/Documents/ent-Breach_Level_Index_Annual_Report_2015.pdf>.

[11] *See id.* at 6.

[12] *See id.* at 3-4.

[13] *See id.* at 2, 12.

[14] *See id.* at 5.

[15] *See* Verizon, *2016 Data Breach Investigations Report: Executive Summary* at 2 (2016), *available online at* <http://www.verizonenterprise.com/resources/reports/rp_dbir-2016-executive-summary_xg_en.pdf>

[16] *Id.* at 10.

[17] *See* Mandiant Consulting, *M-Trends 2016*, at 4 (Feb. 2016), available online at <>.

[18] *Id.*

[19] *See Verizon 2016 DBIR*, n. 15 *supra* at 4.

[20] *Id.* at 6.

[21] *Id.* at 9.

patched. In a 2016 report, Cisco reported that a one-day scan identified 115,000 of its own devices running on the Internet, 92% of which (106,000 devices) had known vulnerabilities in the software they were running.[22] Cisco further determined that these devices were running software that had, on average, 26 vulnerabilities and, in some cases, Cisco found that its customers in the financial, healthcare, and retail sectors using software more than six years old.[23]

And in troubling news for matters under this Committee's jurisdiction, Cisco's 2015 Security Capabilities Benchmark Study found that small and midsize businesses worldwide "show signs that their defenses against attackers are weaker than their challenges demand."[24] Specifically, the Cisco survey found that as compared to 2014, fewer and fewer small and midsize businesses are using web security, mobile security, vulnerability scanning, and patching and configuration tools, and that of the small to midsized businesses without "an executive responsible for security, nearly one-quarter do not believe their businesses are high-value targets for online criminals."[25] Cisco also found, perhaps unsurprisingly, that small and midsize businesses are less likely to have incident response and threat intelligence teams and that such enterprises "use fewer processes [than large enterprises] to analyze compromises, eliminate the causes of an incident, and restore systems to pre-incident levels."[26] Cisco's main point about why all of this matters is also spot on: not only do businesses of all sizes need to take action to protect their own networks, they must be wary of risks they pose to other, sometimes larger, enterprises.[27]

And while the quantity of records estimated to have been lost to nation-state actors may appear relatively small when compared to other malicious outsiders, these numbers do not fully account for the massive scale and scope of intellectual property theft targeting American private sector businesses by nation-state actors or their proxies, principally China. While such theft has been taking place for many years, it has only been openly discussed in the last five years or so. For example, in 2011, former House Intelligence Committee Chairman Mike Rogers famously noted

> There is an economic cyber war going on today against U.S. companies. There are two types of companies in this country, those who know they've been hacked, and those who don't know they've been hacked. Economic predators, including nation-states, are blatantly stealing business secrets and innovation from private companies.[28]

---

[22] *See* Cisco, *Cisco 2016 Annual Security Report* at 35, *available online at* <http://www.cisco.com/c/dam/assets/offers/pdfs/cisco-asr-2016.pdf>.

[23] *Id.*

[24] *Id.* at 37.

[25] *Id.* at 37-38.

[26] *Id.* at 38.

[27] *Id.* at 39 ("In a security environment where attackers are developing more sophisticated tactics for entering networks and remaining undetected, no business can afford to leave its networks unprotected, or to put off using processes that might offer insights on how a compromise occurred so it can be avoided in the future. In addition, SMBs may not realize that their own vulnerability translates to risks for larger enterprise customers and their networks. Today's criminals often gain entry into one network as a means to find an entry point into another, more lucrative network—and the SMB may be the starting point for such an attack.").

[28] *See* House Permanent Select Committee on Intelligence, *Rogers & Ruppersberger Introduce Cybersecurity Bill to Protect American Businesses from "Economic Predators,"* Press Release (Nov. 30, 2011), *available online at* <http://intelligence.house.gov/sites/intelligence.house.gov/files/documents/113011CyberSecurityLegislation.pdf>.

And in July 2012, then-NSA Director Gen. Keith B. Alexander (now retired),[29] referred to the theft of American private sector intellectual property as "the single greatest transfer of wealth in history."[30]

More recently, in September 2015, James Clapper, the Director of National Intelligence, highlighted the ongoing threat posed capable cyber actors, noting that "cyber threats to the U.S. national and economic security are increasing in frequency, scale, sophistication[,] and severity of impact. Although we must be prepared for large Armageddon-scaled strike that would debilitate the entire U.S. infrastructure, that is not, we believe, the most likely scenario."[31] To the contrary, DNI Clapper noted that the intelligence community's primary concerns are the "low to moderate-level cyber-attacks from a variety of sources which will continue and probably expand....[and which] impose[] increasing costs to our business[es], to U.S. economic competiveness[,] and to national security."[32] Deputy Secretary of Defense Bob Work likewise noted that

> [C]yber intrusions and attacks by both state and non-state actors have increased dramatically in recent years, and particularly troubling are the increased frequency and scale of state-sponsored cyber actors breaching U.S. government and business networks. These adversaries continually adapt and evolve in response to our cyber countermeasures, threatening our networks and systems of the Department of Defense, our nation's critical infrastructure[,] and U.S. companies and interests globally.[33]

DNI Clapper also starkly highlighted the risk posed by our increasing reliance on technology and networked devices. In his September 2015 testimony, DNI Clapper noted that "[b]ecause of our heavy dependence on the Internet, nearly all information communication technologies and I.T. networks and systems will be perpetually at risk."[34] DNI Clapper further expanded on this risk in his more recent testimony in February 2016, where he raised concerns about the increasing use of networked devices that are "designed and fielded with minimal security requirements and testing," and noted that reliance on such devices, combined with the "ever-increasing complexity of networks[,] could lead to widespread vulnerabilities in civilian infrastructures and US Government systems."[35]

---

[29] Gen. Alexander currently serves as the President and CEO of IronNet Cybersecurity, the same company employing the author of this testimony.

[30] *See, e.g.,* Josh Rogin, *NSA Chief: Cybercrime Constitutes the "Greatest Transfer of Wealth in History,"* Foreign Policy: The Cable (July 9, 2012), *available online at* <http://foreignpolicy.com/2012/07/09/nsa-chief-cybercrime-constitutes-the-greatest-transfer-of-wealth-in-history/>; *see also* Gen. (ret.) Keith B. Alexander, *Prepared Statement of Gen. (Ret) Keith B. Alexander on the Future of Warfare before the Senate Armed Services Committee* (Nov. 3, 2015) at 3, *available online at* <http://www.armed-services.senate.gov/download/alexander_11-03-15>.

[31] *See* Federal News Service, *Transcript: Hearing Before the Senate Armed Services Committee on Cybersecurity Policy and Threats* at 4 *(Sept. 29, 2015).*

[32] *Id.*

[33] *Id.* at 5-6.

[34] *Id.* at 4.

[35] *See* Director of National Intelligence James R. Clapper, *Statement for the Record: Worldwide Threat Assessment of the US Intelligence Community 2016* at 1, House Permanent Select Committee on Intelligence (Feb. 25, 2016), *available online at* <https://www.dni.gov/files/documents/Newsroom/Testimonies/HPSCI_Unclassified_2016_ATA_SFR-25Feb16.pdf>.

DNI Clapper also highlighted "the targeting of national security information and proprietary information from US companies and research institutions involved with defense, energy, finance, dual-use technology, and other sensitive areas" calling this effort—again principally driven by China—a "persistent threat to US interests" and noted that "[t]he sophistication and availability of information technology that can be used for nefarious purposes exacerbate this threat both in terms of speed and scope of impact."[36]

Key to protecting our nation in cyberspace, therefore, is ensuring the confidentiality, integrity and availability of the information that flows amongst our networked devices. As the DNI noted, this effort to protect our personal and corporate information is under attack from all sides with "cyber espionage [and] criminal and terrorist entities, [] undermin[ing] data confidentiality," with "[d]enial of service operations and data deletion attacks undermin[ing] availability," and an ongoing plague of "cyber operations that [aim to] change or manipulate electronic information [] compromis[ing] its integrity."[37] And, perhaps most concerning of all, we have seen an emergence of actual destructive cyber attacks, that is cyberattacks where cyber or real-world systems, data, or capabilities are permanently destroyed. From the attacks on Saudi Aramco and Qatari Ras Gas in 2012[38] to the attacks on the Las Vegas Sands Corporation and Sony Pictures in 2014,[39] such attacks represent a particularly troubling trend.

Before we turn to how we might work to mitigate the impact of foreign cyber threats on American small businesses, it is worth briefly examining the key foreign threat actors in cyberspace.

IV. Nation-State Threats

The DNI noted in 2015 that "cyber threats come from a range of actors including nation states....with highly sophisticated cyber programs, [such as] Russia and China...And those with lesser technical capabilities but more nefarious intent, such as Iran and North Korea...who are also much more aggressive and unpredictable."[40] And in 2016, the DNI assessed that while both Russia and China "seek

---

[36] *Id.* at 10.

[37] *See Transcript: Cybersecurity Policy and Threats* at 4; *see also Clapper SFR: Worldwide Threat Assessment 2016*, n. 35 *supra* at 2 ("Future cyber operations will almost certainly include an increased emphasis on changing or manipulating data to compromise its integrity (i.e., accuracy and reliability) to affect decisionmaking, reduce trust in systems, or cause adverse physical effects.")

[38] *See* Director of National Intelligence James R. Clapper, *Statement for the Record: Worldwide Threat Assessment of the US Intelligence Community 2013* at 1, Senate Select Committee on Intelligence (Mar. 12, 2013), *available online at* <https://www.dni.gov/files/documents/Intelligence%20Reports/2013%20ATA%20SFR%20for%20SSCI%2012%20Mar%202013.pdf>; Kim Zetter, *Qatari Gas Company Hit With Virus in Wave of Attacks on Energy Companies* (Aug. 30, 2012), *available online at* <https://www.wired.com/2012/08/hack-attack-strikes-rasgas/>.

[39] *See* Director of National Intelligence James R. Clapper, *Opening Statement to Worldwide Threat Assessment Hearing*, Senate Armed Services Committee (Feb. 26, 2015), *available online at* <https://www.dni.gov/files/documents/2015%20WWTA%20As%20Delivered%20DNI%20Oral%20Statement.pdf> ("2014 saw, for the first-time, destructive cyber attacks carried out on U.S. soil by nation state entities, marked first by the Iranian attack on the Las Vegas Sands Casino a year ago this month and the North Korean attack against Sony in November. Although both of these nations have lesser technical capabilities in comparison to Russia and China, these destructive attacks demonstrate that Iran and North Korea are motivated and unpredictable cyber actors.")

[40] *See Transcript: Cybersecurity Policy and Threats*, n. 37 *supra* at 4.

greater influence over their respective neighboring regions and want the United States to refrain from actions they perceive as interfering with their interests" they will also "eschew direct military conflict with the United States in favor of contests at lower levels of competition—to include the use of…cyber intrusions, proxies, and other indirect applications of military power—that intentionally blur the distinction between peace and wartime operations."[41]

Specifically, with respect to Russia, the DNI testified that "Russia is assuming a more assertive cyber posture based on its willingness to target critical infrastructure systems and conduct espionage operations even when detected and under increased public scrutiny."[42] According the DNI, Russian cyber operations are likely to focus on "intelligence gathering to support [their] decision-making in the Ukraine and Syrian crises, influence operations to support military and political objectives, and continuing preparation of the cyber environment for future contingencies."[43] This latter aspect, Russia's ongoing effort to put in place capabilities to be employed in the event of a larger future conflict, should be a major concern for officials in the executive and legislative branches. In particular, this Russian effort to prepare the cyber battlespace ahead of time is particularly concerning given that NSA Director Adm. Mike Rogers has indicated that the Russians are the most "capable" of the nation-state cyber actors targeting the United States.[44]

With respect to China specifically, NSA Director Adm. Mike Rogers has indicated that by the sheer "volume" of data taken, China is the largest cyber actor targeting the United States[45] and the DNI made clear that China "continues to have success in cyber espionage against the US Government, our allies, and US companies."[46] Deputy Secretary of Defense Robert Work has testified that "we believe that Chinese actions in the cyber sphere are totally unacceptable as a nation-state," and has noted that "we know that they have stolen information from our defense contractors."[47] And it goes without saying at this point, that China is the single largest source of data exfiltration—particularly of private sector intellectual property—from the United States.[48] And, it is likewise fair to say that the bulk of this theft is

---

[41] *See* DNI Clapper, *SFR: World Wide Threat Assessment 2016*, n. 35 *supra* at 16.

[42] *Id*. at 3.

[43] *Id*.

[44] See *Transcript: Cybersecurity Policy and Threats*, n. 37 *supra* at 4 ("Unknown: Which country, do you believe, is the most committed, successful hacker of the U.S.? Rogers: If you look at volume and nation-state wise -- nation- state wise, I would -- China, the PRC, has been the one that we've been the most vocal about. They're not the only one by any the stretch of the imagination. Unknown: I thought the last time you were here, I recall you saying that you had more concerns over Russia, having more of the ability or expertise to do us damage. Rogers: I thought your question was really focused more on volume. If the perspective is capability if you will, then we've been very public about saying -- I would probably put the Russians. Unknown: Russians? Rogers: In a higher capability. Unknown: But it seems like that China is more committed and determined to do it. Rogers: They certainly do it at a volume level.")

[45] *Id*.

[46] *Id*. at 3.

[47] *Id*. at 14.

[48] *See* House Permanent Select Committee on Intelligence, *H. Rept. 112-445* (2012) at 5, *available online at* <https://www.congress.gov/112/crpt/hrpt445/CRPT-112hrpt445.pdf> ("Perhaps most troubling, these efforts are targeted not only at sensitive national security and infrastructure information, but are also often aimed at stealing the corporate research and development information that forms the very lifeblood of the American economy. China, in particular, is engaged in an extensive, day-in, day-out effort to pillage American corporate and government information. There can be no question that in today's modern world, economic security is national security, and the government must help the private sector protect itself.");

undertaken by government actors or their proxies, with an eye towards gaining an edge for China in the global marketplace.[49] And, notwithstanding the September 2015 joint commitment between the United States and China to not "conduct or knowingly support cyber-enabled theft of intellectual property, including trade secrets or other confidential business information, with the intent of providing competitive advantages to companies or commercial sectors,"[50] the DNI made clear within days of the deal that he was not optimistic about its prospects.[51]

Moreover, in Feb. 2016, Director Clapper testified that while "[w]e have seen some reduction" in Chinese industrial espionage, in his view, the United States is not "in a position to say at this point whether [China is] in strict compliance."[52] CIA Director John Brennan recently testified that Chinese cyber espionage against American businesses has not ended and that while he "see[s] some effort by the Chinese government to follow through on some of the commitments they've provided in political channels" he "continue[s] to be concerned about the cyber capabilities that reside within China, as well as the actions that some continue to undertake."[53] And while a recent report from FireEye iSight Intelligence indicates a sustained drop-off in the quantity of active network compromises by 72 China-based groups since mid-2014,[54] the report also highlights 13 China-based groups that have actively compromised corporate networks in the U.S., Europe, and Japan between late 2015—after the September 2015 agreement was signed—and early 2016.[55] Indeed, the number of network compromises per month between October 2015 and May 2016, albeit lower than any time in the past two years, has stayed fairly

---

see also House Permanent Select Committee on Intelligence, *Investigative Report on the U.S. National Security Issues Posed by Chinese Telecommunications Companies Huawei and ZTE* (Oct. 8, 2012), *available online at* <https://intelligence.house.gov/sites/intelligence.house.gov/files/documents/Huawei-ZTE%20Investigative%20Report%20(FINAL).pdf> ("Chinese actors are also the world's most active and persistent perpetrators of economic espionage.")

[49] *See id.*

[50] *See* White House, *Fact Sheet: President Xi Jinping's State Visit to the United States* (Sept. 25, 2015), available online at <https://www.whitehouse.gov/the-press-office/2015/09/25/fact-sheet-president-xi-jinpings-state-visit-united-states>.

[51] *See Transcript: Cybersecurity Policy and Threats*, n. 37 *supra* at 8 ("McCain: As a result of the Chinese leader in Washington there was some agreement announced between the United States and China. Do you believe that that will result in an elimination of Chinese cyber attacks? Clapper: Well, hope springs eternal. I think we will have to watch what they're behavior is and it will be incumbent on the intelligence community I think to depict, portray to policymakers what behavioral changes if any, result from this agreement. McCain: Are you optimistic? Clapper: No.")

[52] *See* Federal News Service, *Transcript: Hearing Before the House Permanent Select Committee on Intelligence* at 15 (Feb. 25, 2016) ("Himes: I wonder if you could characterize whether those agreements have been effective in reducing the amount of cyber espionage and cyber activity that we've seen out of China. Clapper: We did probably go into that in more detail on a closed session. As I indicated in my oral remarks, I think the jury's out. We have seen some reduction but I don't think we're in a position to say at this point whether they're in strict compliance. And we can go into that in more detail in a closed session.").

[53] *See* Federal News Service, *Transcript of Hearing Before the Senate Select Committee on Intelligence on CIA Intelligence Activities* at 14 (June 16, 2016) ("Blunt: Let me ask one additional question about China and cyber attacks. Last year, the president announced a common understanding with China's leadership that neither country would conduct, or knowingly support cyber-enabled threat of intellectual property for commercial advantage. In your view, does that mean that cyber-enabled theft of intellectual property by people from china has ended? Brennan: No.").

[54] *See* FireEye iSight Intelligence, *Redline Drawn: China Recalculates Its Use of Cyber Espionage* at 10-11 (June 2016), *available online at* <https://www.fireeye.com/content/dam/fireeye-www/current-threats/pdfs/rpt-china-espionage.pdf>.

[55] *Id.* at 4, 13

constant.[56] That is, while such compromises by China-based actors may have been on a downward trend, ascribing the trend to the September 2015 agreement seems questionable, at best. To the contrary, given that rates have stayed relatively stable since the agreement, one must assume the agreement had limited effect, if any, on China's cyber behavior. As such, while the overall reduction may be laudable, it is unclear whether this truly represents a positive change in behavior or simply evinces a more focused set of cyber activities by China aimed at higher value Western targets.

Another key threat posed by China in the cyber realm, beyond its extremely aggressive policy of cyber theft, is its ostensible effort to obtain access to key U.S. and allied infrastructure. The House Permanent Select Committee on Intelligence, in a report issued in October 2012 after a nearly year long investigation, warned that "[t]he United States should view with suspicion the continued penetration of the U.S. telecommunications market by Chinese telecommunications companies."[57] Specifically, the report recommended that "the Committee on Foreign Investment in the United States (CFIUS) [] block acquisitions, takeovers, or mergers involving [Chinese telecommunications companies] Huawei and ZTE given the threat [these companies pose] to U.S. national security interests."[58] The report further recommended that "U.S. government systems, particularly sensitive systems, should not include Huawei or ZTE equipment, including component parts" and that U.S. "government contractors— particularly those working on contracts for sensitive U.S. programs—should exclude ZTE or Huawei equipment in their systems."[59] Finally, as relevant here, the report recommended that "[p]rivate-sector entities in the United States are strongly encouraged to consider the long-term security risks associated with doing business with either ZTE or Huawei for equipment or services," and stated that, in particular, "U.S. network providers and systems developers are strongly encouraged to seek other vendors for their projects" because "[b]ased on available classified and unclassified information, Huawei and ZTE cannot be trusted to be free of foreign state influence and thus pose a security threat to the United States and to our systems."[60] Given the warnings provided in the HPSCI report, in addition to taking steps to protect themselves against external intrusions, it is important that U.S. businesses—large and small alike—and particularly those in the infrastructure services area, take seriously the potential security threat posed by such companies and take appropriate steps to minimize or otherwise mitigate such risk.

With respect to both Iran and North Korea, the DNI made clear that both are prepared to use cyber to support their political objectives. In the case of Iran, the DNI noted that Iran "used cyber espionage, propaganda, and attacks in 2015 to support its security priorities, influence events, and counter threats— including against US allies in the region."[61] And in the case of North Korea, the DNI made clear his assessment that "North Korea probably remains capable and willing to launch disruptive or destructive cyberattacks to support its political objectives" and specifically noted that South Korea had determined that "North Korea was probably responsible for the compromise and disclosure of data from a South Korean nuclear plant."[62]

---

[56] *Id.* at 11.

[57] *See HPSCI Huawei-ZTE Report*, n. 48 *supra* at vi.

[58] *Id.*

[59] *Id.*

[60] *Id.* at vi-vii.

[61] *See* DNI Clapper, *SFR: World Wide Threat Assessment 2016*, n. 35 *supra* at 3.

[62] *Id.*

V. Non-State Actors

Non-nation state entities also use cyberspace extensively. From organized criminal groups motivated by financial gain and terrorist groups seeking to recruit assets, plan operations, or conduct information operations[63] to hacktivists motivated by ideology and individual criminals or extremists with capable skills, there is no shortage of non-state actors looking to target Americans and their businesses online. In addition to the noting the now run-of-the-mill online marketplaces on the deep- or dark-web where illicit goods and information may be transferred, the DNI recently identified an increasing effort by terrorist groups to experiment as they seek to develop more advanced capabilities.[64] Moreover, the increasing use by criminals of "ransomware" to "block user access to their own data, sometimes by encrypting it, is becoming a particularly effective and popular tool for extortion for which few options for recovery are available" is a significant problem for individuals and businesses alike.[65]

VI. Opportunities to Help Small Business to Protect Themselves

What can small businesses—and the government—do to help address these problems?

First, like large businesses, small businesses must get buy-in for the need for cybersecurity at all levels of the company from the Board of Directors, to the C-suite, and down from there. Such buy-in will help drive appropriate resource allocation decisions that may not otherwise be prioritized. Indeed, Cisco's survey of cybersecurity professionals determined that, regardless the sophistication or cybersecurity maturity of the organization, the single biggest set of obstacles to adopting advanced security processes and technologies were budget constraints, identified as challenges by 38-48% of such professionals.[66]

Second, small businesses must consider working together—for example, within a given industry—to leverage their buying power for cybersecurity services and to take advantage of common services, such as a common security operations center, large scale cyber defense system, and the like.

Third, small businesses must find a way to work with the government and with larger businesses to share cyber threat information in real time, at network speed. Unlike large businesses that may have a fighting chance—albeit it perhaps small—to adequately defend themselves from a committed, capable cyber threat actor, small business are significantly more challenged. And, given the reality of the threat actors targeting American business today, traditional cyber defenses—whether deployed by a large or small business—are ill positioned to respond in a timely and effective fashion.

Fourth, the government must get more serious about deterring nation-state threat actors. To date, our government's ostensibly new, forward-leaning cybersecurity policy has led to one set of symbolic

---

[63] See DNI Clapper, *SFR: World Wide Threat Assessment 2016*, n. 35 *supra* at 3 (highlighting the use of cyberspace by terrorist groups to "organize, recruit, spread propaganda, collect intelligence, raise funds, and coordinate operations" and to conduct information operation campaigns designed to "spur 'lone-wolf' attacks.")

[64] See *Transcript: Cybersecurity Policy and Threats*, n. 27 *supra* at 5.

[65] See DNI Clapper, *SFR: World Wide Threat Assessment 2016*, n. 35 *supra* at 4.

[66] See, e.g., *Cisco 2016 Annual Security Report*, n. 22 *supra* at 51.

indictments—with little chance of an actual trial—a cyber sanctions executive order that has sat unused, and a cyber agreement with China that appears to be being honored in the breach at best. Real deterrence in cyberspace will require the government to be more transparent about its offensive capabilities, to be more clear about the conditions under which it would feel obliged to use such capabilities, and to act on such conditions if they come to pass.

Fifth, the government must work to provide more detailed information about the cyber threats facing our nation to key business and political leaders, including as necessary, providing security clearances and access to information at the TS/SCI level.

Sixth, the government must consider positive incentives—particularly for small businesses—to encourage appropriate investment in cybersecurity and information sharing, including, as appropriate, tax credits for such activities.

Seventh, Congress should consider modifying the Cybersecurity Information Sharing Act of 2015, enacted at the end of last year, in order to provide better incentives for, and to remove barriers to, sharing of cyber threat information.[67]

This short list of ideas represents but a partial starting point for Congress and the private sector to consider going forward in addressing these critical issues.

Thank you for offering me the opportunity to participate in this important dialogue. I look forward to your questions.

---

[67] *See* Jamil N. Jaffer, *Carrots and Sticks in Cyberspace: Addressing Key Issues in the Cybersecurity Information Sharing Act of 2015*, __ S. Car. L. Rev. __ (forthcoming 2016) (describing steps Congress might take to address some of the potential shortcomings in CISA 2015).

Testimony of Justin Zeefe, Small Business Committee, 6 July 2016

Foreign Cyber Threats: Small Business, Big Target

Introduction

Good afternoon and thank you Chairman Chabot and Ranking committee member Velázquez and all Small Business Committee members for the opportunity to testify on foreign cyber threats to American small business.

It is an honor to address members of this distinguished body, both as a small business owner and also as a citizen who notes that small businesses not only employ approximately 50% of the private sector workforce, but they also produce approximately 50% of the non-farming GDP in the United States. They are therefore a vital part economy and their well-begin and the need to ensure their ability to operate in a transport and secure environment is paramount.

My name is Justin Zeefe, and I am co-founder and Chief Strategy Officer of Nisos Group, a cybersecurity firm of former elite cyber operators and Special Forces officers from within the U.S. government. I, and each of my associates, have more than a decade of assessing and mitigating cyber risk to any system which, if compromised, could damage U.S. national security interests. These systems range from critical infrastructure to financial institutions and everything in between. We each observed, over recent years, a significant shift by foreign cyber threats increasingly toward private sector concerns. This evolution, magnified by our observation that the commercial sector is unprepared for the inbound threat, prompted us to bring our capabilities to industry.

It is an honor to speak to you today regarding the most significant present and near-term threat to the national small business economy—foreign cyber threats in the form of cybercrime. There are no shortages of statistics to this end—it is the fastest growing economic crime according to PWC, and is projected to cost the global economy $445 billion by the end of 2016, according to the World Economic Forum. In fact, according to McAfee, the well-renown security company, if cybercrime was a country, its GDP would rank 27th in the world—above Austria, Norway, and Egypt.

How would we collectively react if we knew that the 27th largest economy was absolutely dedicated to attacking our value? What if they were overwhelmingly directing their actions against small businesses? In fact, both of these statements are accurate. Symantec found in June 2015 that 75% of cyberattacks were directed at organizations with fewer than 2,500 employees—a dramatic increase from years prior. Not a week goes by that we don't read of a major data breach in the paper, with mention of what the attackers stole, and often how they managed to gain access.

Most voices and solutions in the field of cybersecurity address the 'what' and 'how' of the threat; yet without an intimate understanding of the threat actors—their motivations, vulnerabilities, capabilities and adaptability—the discussion is incomplete. Never in the history of mankind has there been an industry—illicit or otherwise—which could be addressed strategically without factoring in the players in the game. Cybercrime, and the threat it represents against small businesses and large alike, is no outlier.

This very thing—the 'why'—is a vital part of the equation which requires understanding the humans behind the threat and just as importantly, the vulnerabilities which these threat actors seek to exploit. By understanding the driving forces and motivations behind the threat actors, as well as the evolution of their tools, it is possible to narrow the gap between threat actor capability and the cybersecurity solutions in the marketplace.

Once we understand attacker motivations, it becomes easier to model future behavior from state-sanctioned or state-sponsored activity, and criminal enterprise—the source of almost all cyber incidents. Armed with these insights, only then should we deliberate legislative incentives, penalties, and the appropriate distribution of risk to aid—not hamper—small businesses.

The 'why'

So, why? Why do foreign cyber threats target small businesses? One word and one analogy are sufficient to encapsulate this trend. The word is 'profit' and the analogy is that like water or electricity, malicious hackers follow the path of least resistance. As larger organizations professionalized their defensive and reactive postures to cyber incidents, and as stolen data became less profitable due to a stricter regulatory and law enforcement environment, threat actors—in search of profit—turned their focus to targets which had neither the capacity nor the budget to address cyber threat. A positive feedback loop ensued, in which threat actors only became more dangerous as they adapted to the increasingly sophisticated target set.

The first and most significant evolution was the professionalization of the threat actor. What were only a few years ago best described as small bands of hackers who occasionally work together have, by virtue of their success,, drawn the attention of traditional organized criminal elements. These groups, with many years of experience in the conduct of criminal enterprise, accurately assessed that cybercrime represented an opportunity for increased profit and decreased risk. Rather than trafficking in weapons, drugs or other contraband—activities dependent on physical items which thus present a significant risk of detection or interdiction—these groups of experienced criminals increasingly invest in individuals or groups whose cybercrime activities are both wildly successful and stealthy when it comes to attribution.

The second most significant evolution, inextricably linked to the first, has been the dramatically improved defensive posture of larger organizations. These whales were the first to be targeted and given their deep pockets, they were also the first to fund an improved posture informed by a corporate hierarchy which lends itself to coordinated risk mitigation as well as a keen awareness that the regulatory and judicial systems track their behavior. This evolutionary development is in part driven organically within an organization as well as the result of free market products and services which address the technical problem.

A third and critical component, which is less of an evolution than it is a failure to evolve, deserves consideration here. Small businesses underestimate the degree to which they are vulnerable and they often believe—in the face of plain evidence—that they aren't a legitimate target of cybercriminals. A 2015 survey by the National Small Business Association found that half the respondents had been knowingly targeted, and that the average cost to remediate was more than $20,000. Nevertheless, a report by Travelers Insurance found that only 23% of small businesses "worried a great deal" about cyber risk. In addition to willfully ignoring the first-degree risks, there are often larger secondary risks presented by a vulnerable small business. They are often service providers or vendors to larger businesses and often are, to reuse the analogy, the path of least resistance by which malicious actors can gain unauthorized access to larger organizations.

These two evolutions, along with small business' failure to adapt, readily explains the explosive growth of successful ransomware attacks. If you will permit another analogy, imagine thieves targeting the Louvre museum. Now imagine that a year ago, they could have easily gotten in and stolen the Mona Lisa, which they could have then sold on the black market for millions of dollars. Now consider, much like big business in the United States, that the Louvre has upgraded its security. At the same time, law enforcement has gotten much better at policing the black market. As a consequence, the costs associated with both stealing and reselling the painting exceed the potential benefit. To this, the thieves realize they can simply padlock the entire museum shut, wire all of the art with explosives, and demand payment to disarm the explosives and unlock the doors. Now imagine the costs of conducting this sort of attack were low and could be conducted against thousands of museums in an hour, and that the fee charged to remove the padlock was tens of thousands of dollars—a significant sum but acceptable when compared with the reputational cost of losing revenue or reputation by going public with the incident or by refusing to comply. A dramatic example perhaps, but considering the havoc that ransomware is, at this very moment, causing predominantly to small business, it is not an ill-fitting example.

Conclusion

While understanding the motivations which drive the threat actors is not on its own sufficient to build an effective framework for deterring or interdicting cyberattacks targeting small business, it is a vital component of the problem which cannot be ignored and which needs to be prioritized alongside other more established business risks. When taken in consideration with other factors—such as the advancement of technical solutions (both offensive and defensive)—the knowledge of the enemy and their tactics, techniques and plans may permit a logical and cohesive approach to the ever-evolving problem.

House Committee on Small Business

"Foreign Cyber Threats: Small Business, Big Target"

Testimony of Nova Daly

Senior Policy Advisor, Wiley Rein LLP, Washington, DC

July 6, 2016

Chairman Chabot, Ranking Member Velá zquez, and members of the Committee, thank you for the opportunity to appear before you today.[1]

In this age of the Internet, we have never had so much opportunity and with it so much risk. Today, I offer my perspective on cyber security, broadly, and distinctly as it pertains to small businesses. This perspective is drawn from my experience as a former official with the U.S. Department of Treasury administering the Committee on Foreign Investment in the United States ("CFIUS"), work at the National Security Council, and my ongoing efforts in the private sector with my colleagues at Wiley Rein to address these issues as they impact U.S. companies.

As this Committee knows, cyber security issues are clearly significant and growing economic risks for small business and Americans broadly. These issues have become increasingly relevant as we now allow and depend upon Internet access and connectivity in nearly every aspect of our work and lives, from the communication and processing devices we use at home and work, to the vehicles we drive, the infrastructure on which we depend, and even the appliances in our homes.

It has been forecast that, on average, 5.5 million new devices are connected to the Internet each day and, by 2020, over 20 billion devices will be connected to the Internet.[2] For small businesses, they very connectivity that allows greater freedom and versatility in conducting day-to-day business—linking phones, computers, routers, copiers, and even alarm and ventilation systems—also brings with it significant and sometimes paralyzing risk, risk that is often difficult to address both financially and in terms of human resources.

As small businesses increase their connectivity to the Internet, they face significant challenges and additional costs, not just in infrastructure and the 'nuts and bolts' of establishing businesses' connectivity, but also security-related costs. Both domestic and foreign criminals, as well as foreign governments, have been known to exploit and are actively targeting internet-based vulnerabilities in order to gain access to financial information, customer data, and

---

[1] The views and opinions expressed in this statement are mine and do not necessarily reflect the views or opinions of Wiley Rein LLP or any of its clients.
[2] *See* http://www.gartner.com/newsroom/id/3165317

intellectual property. Indeed, three years ago, a study issued by the Center for Strategic and International Studies estimated that the annual cost of cybercrime in the United States was approximately $100 billion. According to more recent reports, cybercrime costs quadrupled since then, and we are on target for still another quadrupling of these costs from 2015 to 2019.

While large U.S. businesses typically have the means to fund and invest in strong and resi8lient cyber security measures to protect their interests, small businesses generally do not have this luxury. They often lack the capabilities and/or the resources to pursue strong, entity-wide cyber security protections. Further, small businesses often may not be privy to the kinds of broad, industry-wide threat notifications to which larger companies may be. Often, larger companies have the resources to continually monitor and review threats that may arise from certain technology and supply chains, and at times are contacted by the U.S. government when breaches occur. A notable example was the 2014 Department of Justice investigation and prosecution of several Chinese military officials, who were responsible for breaches of numerous U.S. companies' security perimeters. There, at least some of the affected companies were contacted and alerted as the breaches were occurring. However, given the breadth of existing cyber threats and the continuing growth of cybercrime, our government simply does not have the resources to address all of the cyber security-related issues faced by business, critical infrastructure, and governmental systems, much less those faced by small businesses.

In 2012, the House Permanent Select Committee on Intelligence issued a report on its finding regarding counterintelligence and security threats posed by certain telecommunications companies doing business in the United States. Despite the report's negative findings, the companies investigated continue to grow as dominant players in the global telecommunications market. While it has been effectively restricted from selling network equipment to tier-one U.S. wireless carriers, Huawei is growing its sales to smaller wireless carriers in the United States, supplying network infrastructure equipment to cities in the states of Washington and Oregon, and is targeted to continue growth in cell phone sales in the U.S. market. Last year, ZTE another of the investigated companies, was the fourth-largest smartphone vendor in the United States, with a 7.2% market share. In the fourth quarter of last year, the single largest market for ZTE smartphones was the United States. These companies also sell tablets, routers, hotspots, data storage, and cloud computing infrastructure and services, all of which are used by small businesses.

Although larger U.S. companies can engage other vendors to provide certain cyber security monitoring and reinforcement of their security perimeters, small businesses often do not have the funds or capacity to do so. Notably, this year, ZTE was sanctioned, and according to reports, Huawei has been subpoenaed by the U.S. Department of Commerce for potential violations of U.S. export laws in sending controlled items to countries that have been designated as supporters of international terrorism, or are otherwise subject to

U.S. trade sanctions and economic embargoes, such as Cuba, Iran, North Korea, Sudan, and Syria.

While doing business with such companies can present heightened risk, it should not be overlooked that there is significant and growing vulnerability within the entire U.S. technology supply chain. Increasingly, our telecommunications equipment and systems are produced or assembled abroad, and we are seeing nations taking strong measures to grow their own semiconductor and other technology industries. Further, the United States is finding itself with a talent shortage in cybersecurity know-how. Thus, there are also broader structural problems that should be closely addressed. Cyber security or insecurity, as compounded for small business, does have a correlation to the capability of our cyber work force and security of our entire technology supply chains.

So how do we ensure that small businesses are not left to fend for themselves in an increasingly hostile cyber world? For the consideration of this Committee I respectfully submit the following recommendations.

A focus on current laws. A continued focus on the enforcement of our export control, cyber and other national security laws, such as CFIUS, is appropriate. Understandably, when implementing restrictions that prohibit exports, reexports, and transfers (in-country) of items subject to the punitive action, an administration must take into consideration the broader effects that such actions will cause. However, ensuring that our laws are enforced against those who violate them sends important signals to the market. Such signals can make their way to small businesses, allowing them to be better served through purchases of products by vendors who follow the laws.

Promoting cyber standards. This Committee should continue to consider actions that build and promote industry-led cyber security standards in the framework of ISO standards, or otherwise, of best practice. Such standards could be applied to government procurement, ensuring that government agencies access equipment from vendors that achieve acceptable standards of cyber security protection. Doing so could ensure that such equipment permeates to the private sector broadly and especially to small business. Agencies such as the Small Business Administration could help to educate small businesses on these standards so that they are aware of where best to turn for equipment and services that reduce their cyber risk.

Engaging small businesses. Increasing outreach and education to small businesses and finding appropriate funding so that they are aware of the risks to their systems and have the means to address that risk could be pursued. As part of those efforts, it would be useful to strengthen information-sharing initiatives between entities in order to provide small businesses with a more immediate understanding of emerging threats and patterns, and arm these businesses with the lessons learned from others. We could also consider ways to build incentives for purchasing safer equipment. Such market-based cyber incentives, whether in purchasing, insurance, or otherwise would help justify investments in cyber security. Profit-minded organizations must see clear benefits to their actions, as every dollar or hour spent on cyber security is not spent on the organization's core goals. These actions accompanied with industry norms and standards could highlight cyber security investments as requisite. Passage of H.R. 5064, The Improving Small Business Cyber Security Act of 2016, would be important to these ends.

Addressing supply chain security issues and closing the cyber deficit. As noted earlier, given the global nature of technology production and cyber threats, we must find ways to address the threats that emanate from these supply chains. While important work is being done in the government and private sector to find and achieve the right answers, this should continue to be a focus of U.S. policy. Toward that end, and as has been widely reported, we have a troubling cyber deficit in terms of talent and training here in the United States. We need to build the next generation of cyber technicians and engineers. If we do not build this capacity, it will be sourced from abroad, and doing so could put us behind the technology and innovation curve. One element that makes America strong is our ability to innovate, and that comes with building the next technologies. We need to reclaim that field.

Thank you very much again for the opportunity to testify before this Committee today on this important topic. I look forward to answering any questions that you may have.

Testimony of Angela Dingle

On behalf of

Women Impacting Public Policy

Submitted to the

House Small Business Committee

"Foreign Cyber Threats: Small Business, Big Target"

July 6, 2016

Good afternoon. Chair Chabot, Ranking Member Velazquez and distinguished Members of the Committee, thank you for the opportunity to testify. My name is Angela Dingle. I am the President and CEO of Ex Nihilo, a women-owned small business, based in Washington, DC that provides cyber security, governance and risk management services to government agencies.

I am here today representing Women Impacting Public Policy (WIPP) where I serve as Chair of its Education Foundation. WIPP is a national nonpartisan public policy organization advocating on behalf of its coalition of 4.7 million businesswomen including 78 business organizations.

First, let me thank the Committee for holding this hearing. WIPP is appreciative of the bipartisan efforts of this Committee to advance the agenda of women entrepreneurs including accessing capital, accessing federal markets, and providing a business friendly environment.

Few topics are as timely as today's hearing: the proliferating danger of cyber threats and their impact on the small business community. Witnesses today will share statistics that portray a ubiquitous threat facing businesses of all sizes—the most devastating impact on smaller firms. In a hearing earlier this year, the Committee noted, "The outcome of an attack can be catastrophic for small business owners because many firms are unable to recover from the loss of their intellectual property or resources."[1] That conclusion is borne out by findings from the National Cyber Security Alliance that 60% of small businesses will close within six months of a cyber attack.[2]

Narrowing the focus, businesses that work with the federal government are an additional security risk as U.S. Government data is of high value to individuals, companies, and governments across the world. Due to increasing privacy requirements and recent cyber-attacks, the Department of Defense (DOD) has responded by implementing new technical and contractual requirements for contractors doing business with them.

My testimony will focus on these new regulations and their potential threated the nearly 75,000 women-owned firms engaged with the federal government. WIPP is particularly concerned about the significant cost associated with these requirements and their potential to push women-owned firms out of the federal marketplace – only months after reaching the 5% goal for the first time[3].

---

[1] House Committee on Small business, (2016, April 20). Hearing Memo: Small Business, Big Threat: Protecting Small Businesses from Cyber Attacks. Retrieved July 1, 2016, from http://smallbusiness.house.gov/uploadedfiles/4-22-2015_updatedmemo.pdf

[2] New Survey Shows U.S. Small Business Owners Not Concerned About Cybersecurity; Majority Have No Policies or Contingency Plans. Retrieved July 1, 2016, from https://staysafeonline.org/about-us/news/new-survey-shows-us-small-business-owners-not-concerned-about-cybersecurity

[3] SBA: Federal Government Breaks Contracting Record for Women-Owned Small Businesses | The U.S. Small Business Administration | SBA.gov. (2016, March). Retrieved July 1, 2016, from

Defense Federal Acquisition Regulation Supplement Clause 252.204-7012

In August 2015, the DOD finalized a Defense Federal Acquisition Regulation (DFAR), requiring companies of all sizes to safeguard Unclassified Controlled Technical Information (UCTI) that resides on their information systems.[4] Controlled technical information is defined as technical data or computer software with military or space application that is subject to controls on the access, use, reproduction, modification, performance, display, release, disclosure, or dissemination and is marked in accordance with DOD instructions.

To follow this rule, a federal contractor is required to be compliant with National Institute of Standards and Technology (NIST) Special Publication (SP) 800-171 – guidelines for "Protecting Controlled Unclassified Information in Nonfederal Information Systems and Organizations." The goal is to provide minimum standards to protect government information that finds its way into contractor information systems.

These guidelines have been tailored for private entities including contractors and research institutions. They include 14 "families" of security requirements (commonly known as security controls or security objectives) that must be satisfied. These groupings range from identification and authentication to physical protection.

Contractors that do not implement safeguards for the 14 "families", must submit a written explanation of why the required security control is not applicable, or explain how an alternative control or protective measure is being used to achieve the same level of protection.

Due to the high compliance burden of this new policy, the Defense Department revised the rule in December 2015, to give contractors additional time to implement the security requirements by December 31, 2017. While giving businesses additional time to comply may be helpful, it is clear from speaking with other small contractors many do not have the resources to comply with this rule.

This past February, the SBA office of Advocacy found that the DOD rule grossly underestimated the number of affected small businesses[5]. DOD's estimates only included small business prime contractors, though the rule extends to tens of thousands of small business subcontractors in the federal supply chain.

---

https://www.sba.gov/content/sba-federal-government-breaks-contracting-record-women-owned-small-businesses

[4]Guidance to Stakeholders for Implementing Defense Federal Acquisition Regulation Supplement Clause 252.204-7012 (Safeguarding Unclassified Controlled Technical Information). (2015, August). Retrieved July 1, 2016, from http://www.acq.osd.mil/se/docs/DFARS-guide.pdf

[5] Interim Rule, Defense Federal Acquisition Supplement: Network Penetration Reporting and Contracting for Cloud Services | The U.S. Small Business Administration | SBA.gov. (2016, February 29). Retrieved July 05, 2016, from https://www.sba.gov/advocacy/2-29-16-interim-rule-defense-federal-acquisition-supplement-network-penetration-reporting

The Office of Advocacy recommended that the Defense Department collaborate with universities and other organizations to provide low-cost cybersecurity services to small businesses participating in the federal acquisition process or provide a one-time subsidy to small contractors participating in the acquisition process to cover the cost of consultations with third-party vendors. The Office of Advocacy also found that the cost of compliance with this rule will be a significant barrier to small businesses engaging in the federal acquisition process.

While all 14 "families" of security controls may not apply to every company, the standards are clear that information security is not just for information technology contractors like myself. Understanding and managing information security risks can be challenging, especially for companies that are not in the business of cyber security.

National Industrial Security Operating Manual Conforming Change 2

Even more concerning than the recent change to the DFAR is the May 18, 2016 National Industrial Security Operating Manual Conforming Change 2[6], commonly referred to as the "Insider Threat Program." The regulation stems directly from concerns over foreign actors using federal employees to bypass security safeguards. This regulation requires contractors gather, integrate, and report relevant credible information that may indicate an insider threat.

It is especially burdensome for small businesses because it has to be implemented by November 30, 2016 and for the first time, the Defense Department is requiring businesses to appoint a senior level W2 employee to serve as Insider Threat Program Senior Official (ITPSO). The ITPSO must serve in a position within the company that has the authority to provide management, accountability and oversight for implementation of the insider threat program.

For some women-owned businesses, this means they have to hire additional personnel to comply with this requirement. Additionally, in order to adequately report compliance with this regulation, women-owned businesses may have to invest in technology to assist them in detecting, analyzing and reporting on insider threats.

Cyber Security and the Small Business Community

Lack of technical knowledge is not an excuse for failure to comply with basic cyber security regulations. While it may be difficult for individuals without a technical background to understand the intricacies of these new guidelines, small businesses need to proactively do the following:

---

[6] Defense Security Service Industrial Security Letter ISL 2016-02. (2016, May 21). Retrieved July 1, 2016, from http://www.dss.mil/documents/isp/ISL2016-02.pdf

- Understand the scope and impact of changes on the business
- Align organizational policies, practices and procedures to comply
- Empower those with the technical expertise necessary
- Provide adequate training to ensure employees are aware of their responsibilities
- Hold individuals accountable for compliance

Unless properly managed, information security compliance can be a very costly proposition. Companies that do not have a solid understanding of information technology and information security find themselves reacting to an ever-changing sea of regulatory requirements that will be costly to implement.

While many small businesses are looking to the cloud and its host of services as a way of managing costs, doing so without understanding the security implications can increase the company's security posture to an unacceptable risk level.

New contract guidelines require a small business to rethink an existing product, service, or process, thereby introducing unplanned costs. Management needs to understand the scope of security requirements and ensure that they are incorporated into buying decisions, product and services contracts, service level agreements and human resources processes.

The first step is to get a jumpstart on the new requirements by assessing current information systems and determining changes necessary for compliance with new guidelines. Implementing effective governance processes can help small businesses manage information security risk, increase stakeholder confidence and reduce the costs associated with compliance.

To that end, small businesses could use assistance in determining their cyber security needs. WIPP supports the intent of H.R. 5064, the *Improving Small Business Cyber Security Act of 2016*[7] introduced by Representative Richard Hanna, which was included in this year's defense authorization. The legislation authorizes Small Business Development Centers (SBDC) to support small businesses in developing affordable cyber security plans. However, we would encourage the Committee to consider adding other SBA resource partners, including over 100 Women's Business Centers to do this outreach.

In conclusion, women entrepreneurs consider the federal marketplace a key opportunity to grow their businesses. With more than ten million women business owners nationwide, competition for government opportunities among women innovators and entrepreneurs remains strong. While there is a need to protect federal data, and small businesses need to protect themselves from cyber attacks, the government has gone too far with these new regulations. One size does not fit all. Ensuring that new cyber security requirements are attainable for small businesses is of paramount importance. This Committee has always

---

[7] H.R. 5064 Improving Small Business Cyber Security Act of 2016. Retrieved July 1, 2016, https://www.congress.gov/bill/114th-congress/house-bill/5064/text?q=%7B%22search%22%3A%5B%22Improving+Small+Business+Cyber+Security+Act+of%22%5D%7D&resultIndex=1

acted in a bipartisan manner to support women entrepreneurs and we appreciate your examination of this issue, making sure that these requirements achieve the desired results, rather than more red tape.

Thank you for the opportunity to testify and I am happy to answer any questions.

1776 K STREET NW
WASHINGTON, DC 20006
PHONE 202.719.7000
FAX 202.719.7049

7925 JONES BRANCH DRIVE
McLEAN, VA 22102
PHONE 703.905.2800
FAX 703.905.2820

www.wileyrein.com

August 11, 2016

Nova J. Daly
202.719.3282
ndaly@wileyrein.com

VIA ELECTRONIC MAIL

The Honorable Grace Meng
Committee on Small Business
2361 Rayburn House Office Building
Washington, DC 20515

Dear Congresswoman Meng,

Thank you very much for your follow-up questions for the record ("QFRs") initiated in connection with the House Committee on Small Business's "Foreign Cyber Threats: Small Business, Big Target" hearing held on July 6, 2016. It was an honor and privilege to be able to present my testimony to the Committee, and I respectfully provide my responses to your QFRs below following text excerpts from your QFR transmission of July 18, 2016. Please note that, as was true of my testimony, the views and opinions expressed in this response are mine alone; they do not necessarily reflect the views or opinions of my employer, Wiley Rein LLP, or any of its clients.

Thank you again for the opportunity to submit additional information in response to your QFRs. Should you have any questions or require any further information in connection with the responses presented in this submission, please do not hesitate to contact me.

Respectfully submitted,

Nova J. Daly
Senior Policy Advisor

Enclosure

14015933.4

1.) **There have been calls from some of my colleagues for the Department of Commerce to restrict exports of U.S. technology suppliers to foreign firms over cybersecurity concerns. Would it be wise to ban all such exports, and what would the impact be upon the U.S. economy and U.S. companies? With respect to China specifically, isn't doing business with the largest economy on the planet desirable?**

The United States already has in place laws and regulations governing and controlling the exportation of U.S. technology to foreign customers. These longstanding rules – among them the Export Administration Regulations ("EAR") and International Traffic in Arms Regulations ("ITAR") – allow U.S. suppliers to conduct international commerce and trade while protecting certain national security interests. Indeed, our firm has considerable experience in helping companies navigate U.S. export control regimes. We understand that the U.S. government's decision to limit the export of any specific technology or item is made with careful consideration as to both the national security interests that are potentially exposed by such transactions as well as the impact of that limitation on U.S. businesses and their global partners and customers.

The U.S. government does impose export controls on some technology and items and their provision to certain foreign parties. Such controls are generally implemented on a product-and/or case-specific basis, and some of these restrictions apply to individuals and entities who have been found to have committed violations of the United States' existing export rules. These controls, however, in no way constitute a complete "ban" on all exports of technology and technology items to all customers abroad, including Chinese customers.

2.) **Historically, China has promoted policies that encourage replacing American technology with Chinese products. The U.S. government and industry have continually opposed such policies, but it sounds today as if some of my colleagues are clamoring to block Chinese companies from engaging the American market. Is it wise to encourage the Chinese market to look elsewhere when it comes to procuring technological components for their manufactured goods? If China domestically produced all of the components its companies needed, what impact would that have on the U.S economy?**

With regard to China's promotion of policies that encourage replacing American technology with Chinese products, I thank you for calling out and recognizing the perils of indigenous innovation. Several years ago, the Chinese government embarked on a campaign of development and growth driven by a program of indigenous innovation, among other factors. China's and other nations' indigenous innovation policies broadly seek the advancement of domestic technological prowess through "co-innovation and re-innovation based on the assimilation of imported technologies."[1] It is this coopting of foreign-developed (*i.e.*, U.S.-developed) technology that has led the U.S. government to encourage China to reevaluate its

---

[1] James McGregor, "China's Drive for 'Indigenous Innovation': A Web of Industrial Policies," Global Regulatory Cooperation Project, U.S. Chamber of Commerce (July 2010) at 4, *citing* China's "National Medium- and Long-Term Plan for the Development of Science and Technology (2006-2020)."

10

implementation of such policies and to abide by certain basic and common international rules and practices with regard to unfair trade practices.[2]

With regard to your question concerning the "blocking" of Chinese companies from engaging the American market, I am unsure of what, specifically, you are referencing. I can, however, provide examples where issues of market access have been raised concerning certain Chinese entities.

In 2012, after investigation, the U.S. House Permanent Select Committee on Intelligence issued a report that identified Chinese telecommunications companies Huawei Technologies ("Huawei") and ZTE Corporation ("ZTE") as potential threats to national security, given the two entities' close ties to the Chinese government.[3] As a result of its investigation, the Select Committee strongly encouraged U.S. private-sector entities to seek other vendors for their telecommunications equipment and service needs.[4] Huawei and ZTE are two of China's largest and farthest-reaching telecommunications entities, and both have significant international market success.

Recently, in March of this year, the U.S. Department of Commerce's Bureau of Industry and Security ("BIS") imposed restrictions on exports to ZTE of all technology and other items subject to the EAR in response to ZTE's re-exportation of controlled items to Iran, a practice which is contrary to U.S. national security and foreign policy and constitutes a violation of U.S. export control laws.[5] While those restrictions have since been relaxed,[6] the example of ZTE stands as a reminder of the U.S. government's ability to enforce its export controls rules. Further, according to reports, in June of this year, BIS issued a subpoena to Huawei regarding potential transactions involving sanctioned countries such as Cuba, Iran, North Korea, Sudan and Syria.

The United States has laws, including export controls that have been established to protect U.S. national security interests. Violators of these laws, both foreign and domestic, are subject to enforcement actions.

With regard to your question concerning the impact on the U.S. economy should China pursue domestic production of all technology components currently sourced from U.S.

---

[2] *See, e.g.,* Ben Rhodes, Deputy National Security Advisor, *et al.*, Press Briefing on the Upcoming Visit of Chinese Vice President Xi Jinping to the United States (Feb. 10, 2012), *available at* https://www.whitehouse.gov/the-press-office/2012/02/10/press-briefing-upcoming-visit-chinese-vice-president-xi-jinping-united-s.

[3] *See* Investigative Report on the U.S. National Security Issues Posed by Chinese Telecommunications Companies Huawei and ZTE, U.S. House of Representatives, 112th Congress (Oct. 8, 2012), *available at* https://intelligence.house.gov/sites/intelligence.house.gov/files/documents/huawei-zte%20investigative%20report%20(final).pdf.

[4] *See id.* at 45.

[5] *See Additions to the Entity List,* 81 Fed. Reg. 12,004 (Dep't Commerce Mar. 8, 2016) (final rule).

[6] *See Temporary General License,* 81 Fed. Reg. at 15,633 (Dep't Commerce Mar. 24, 2016) (final rule); *Temporary General License: Extension of Validity,* 81 Fed. Reg. 41,799 (Dep't Commerce June 28, 2016) (final rule).

companies, I regret that I am unable to provide any concrete data points as I am not an economist sufficiently well versed in such matters. Further, as I noted in my testimony, Wiley Rein is a firm that deals with the legal aspects of export controls and, as such, does not collect or maintain data specific to your question.

3.)   Many small businesses are particularly vulnerable to cybercrime. Oftentimes, they do not have the necessary resources to continuously protect themselves, their employees, or their customers against identity theft, intellectual property theft, etc. What can we, the U.S. government, do to provide greater assistance to small businesses as they seek to protect themselves from cyber-criminals? Are our current laws sufficient to enable the federal government to protect small businesses from cybercrime?

Thank you for your question concerning what support the U.S. government can provide to small businesses struggling to keep pace with and protect themselves against constantly evolving cybersecurity threats. As I and others testified at the hearing, there are multiple ways in which the U.S. government can provide greater assistance to small businesses, including the following:

- *Focusing on current laws.* The U.S. government should continue to focus on and make a priority the enforcement of our export and other cybersecurity and national security laws, such as those bolstering CFIUS. Ensuring that our existing laws are enforced sends important signals not only to those who would engage in violations, but also to other market actors. And, through the market, such signals can make their way to small businesses and influence their purchasing patterns to incorporate purchases from vendors who uphold and follow the relevant laws.
- *Education of small businesses on cybersecurity best practices and standards.* Congress and agencies like the Small Business Administration could help to educate small businesses on prevailing and developing cybersecurity and other privacy standards to help these entities develop functional, ground-level facility with such concepts and emphasize the importance of greater vigilance with regard to cybersecurity threats, both to individual companies and to the greater small business community. This education could also include information on how to acquire and where to turn for equipment and services that can reduce cyber risk.
- *Promotion of cyber standards.* Congress should continue to encourage industry-led development of cybersecurity standards, mirroring the framework of ISO standards of best practice. Such standards, once established, could also benefit the government procurement process, ensuring that government agencies procure equipment from vendors that can maintain acceptable levels of cybersecurity protection. In encouraging the establishment of such a framework, Congress would help to ensure that reliance on secure systems and equipment would also permeate private sector transactions, both with regard to small businesses as well as on a broader scale.
- *Closing the cyber deficit.* We as a nation are currently suffering a troubling deficit in terms of cybersecurity talent and training. We need to build the next generation of cyber technicians and engineers, not simply import them. Innovation has long been the strong suit of American industry, and we should continue to claim that field by growing and encouraging our cybersecurity and technology workforce.

As to the state of our current cybercrime laws, I would encourage the U.S. government to tailor its legislative approach to cybercrime to the fluid and ever-changing nature of technology. As technology advances and evolves, so too must the laws governing and surrounding it.

ROBERT PITTENGER
MEMBER OF CONGRESS
9TH DISTRICT, NORTH CAROLINA

224 CANNON HOUSE OFFICE BUILDING
WASHINGTON, DC 20515
(202) 225-1976
FAX (202) 225-3389

COMMITTEES
FINANCIAL SERVICES

Congress of the United States
House of Representatives
Washington, DC 20515–3309

DISTRICT OFFICES
2701 Coltsgate Road
Suite 105
CHARLOTTE, NC 28211
(704) 365-6234
FAX (704) 365-6384

116 MORLAKE DRIVE
SUITE 101A
MOORESVILLE, NC 28117
(704) 696-8188
FAX (704) 696-8190

July 6, 2016

The Honorable Steve Chabot
Chairman
House Small Business Committee
Washington, D.C.

Dear Mr. Chairman,

Thank you for allowing me to participate at your cybersecurity hearing earlier this afternoon. I would like to submit the following opening statement for the record.

"Good afternoon Mr. Chairman and thank you for hosting me today to discuss foreign cyber threats and how they affect the private sector.

Cybersecurity threats come in many forms, and developing an adequate countermeasure strategy can be complex and involve a multitude of disciplines.

One area where both the government and private sector can improve is supply chain security.

As many are aware, the Chinese government remains the number one state-sponsor of cyber-espionage and intellectual property theft in the world.

Yet, there are many businesses in China, often affiliated with the Chinese government, that are multi-billion dollar private sector vendors which produce IT components that are sold to both the U.S. government and private sector.

If we are aware of China's aggressive cyberespionage activities, then how can we justify purchasing sensitive technological equipment from a company that is owned or affiliated with the Chinese government?

With that in mind, the federal government must lead by example.

The federal government has access to vast amounts of intelligence information that the private sector simply does not have, therefore, when our government becomes aware of a supply chain risk, it is imperative that we take swift and affirmative action to remove such a company as a vendor.

This not only strengthens the government's security, but it sends a strong message to private sector entities who may think twice before doing business with a company that is denied by the federal government.

I applaud your leadership in hosting this hearing, and I look forward to working with you to ensure that both the federal government and private sector have the information and capabilities necessary to combat foreign cybersecurity threats."

Sincerely,

Robert Pittenger
Member of Congress